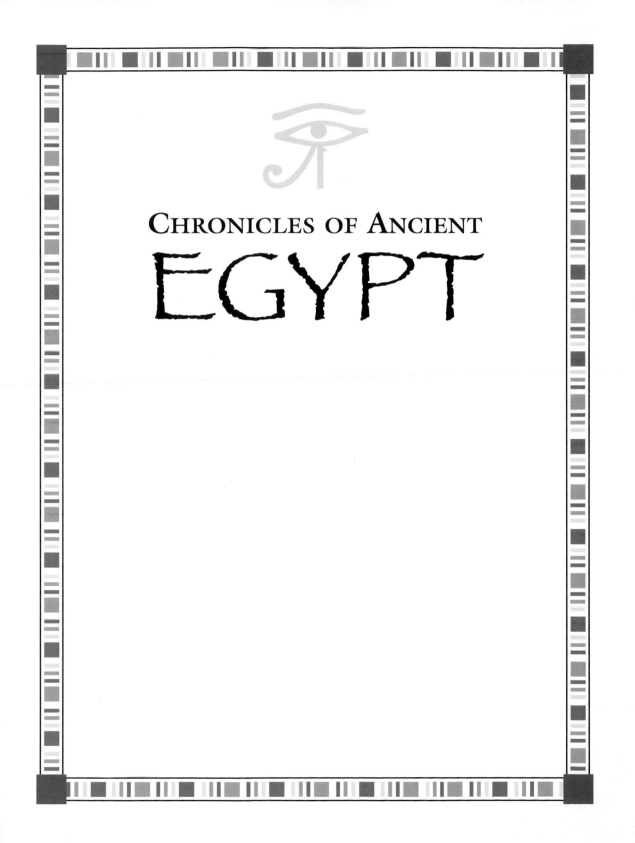

CHRONICLES OF ANCIENT

EGYPT

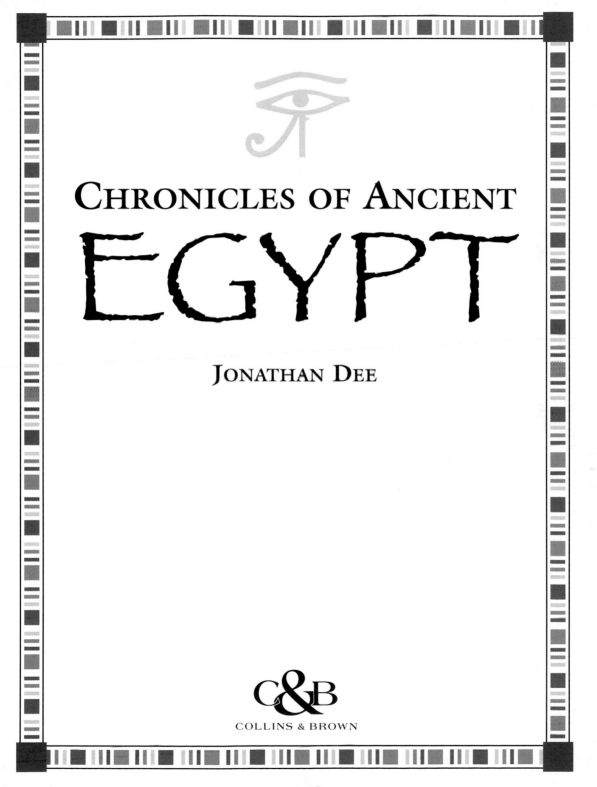

CHRONICLES OF ANCIENT
EGYPT

JONATHAN DEE

C&B

COLLINS & BROWN

DEDICATION
TO SASHA,
and also to those who have gone to dwell in the West

AUTHOR'S ACKNOWLEDGEMENTS
With gratitude for the encouragement given by Jan Budkowski, Grant Griffiths, Russell Spinola, Liz Dean, Jamie Withey, Julian Maher and Susan Martineau during the production of this book.

First published in Great Britain in 1998 by Collins & Brown Ltd
London House
Great Eastern Wharf
Parkgate Road
London SW11 4NQ

Copyright © Collins & Brown Limited 1998
Text copyright © Jonathan Dee 1998

The right of Jonathan Dee to be identified as the author of this work has been asserted by him in accordance with the Copyright, Designs and Patents Act, 1988.

A CIP catalogue record of this book is available from the British Library.

ISBN 1-85585-606-9 (hb)
ISBN 1-85585-659-X (pb)

1 3 5 7 9 8 6 4 2

Project Editor: Susan Martineau
Designer: Alison Lee

Editorial Director: Sarah Hoggett
Art Director: Roger Bristow

Picture Research: Philippa Lewis
Artworks and Cover Design: Alison Lee

Colour reproduction: Hong Kong Graphic and Printing, Hong Kong
Printed by: Midas, Hong Kong

CONTENTS

INTRODUCTION

THE ENDURING FASCINATION of the Land of the Pharaohs has cast a potent spell over people of all historical ages. We, like Julius Caesar, are as captivated by the magic and mysteries of the land of the Nile as he was by the charms of the sultry Cleopatra. The almost incredible antiquity of the surviving monuments gives us the feeling that we stand next to Caesar in time while figures such as Ramesses the Great and the Pharoah Khufu recede into the remote distance, leaving only enigmatic memorials of stone to tantalize our imaginations.

The fall of the Roman Empire took the culture and knowledge of Ancient Egypt with it. As the temple of Isis at Philae fell, so did the last repository of the wisdom of those priests and scribes who had maintained their civilization for more than 3,000 years. The troublesome centuries which followed cast a shadow over the gods of the Ancient Egyptians as new religions superseded them and as the encroaching desert sands overwhelmed their temples and monuments, burying them from sight and memory.

In 1798 a new empire-builder, Napoleon Bonaparte, invaded Egypt. Like Caesar and Alexander before him, he was fascinated by the colossal memorials of ancient times, and brought with him scholars to study the mighty remnants of the fallen pharaohs. After a gap of almost 2,000 years, Egypt again captured the interest of Europe and Ancient Egyptian styles found their way into Regency drawing-rooms. Yet this renewed attention had some tragic consequences; after all, no native Egyptian would have dreamed of using the nose of the Great Sphinx for target practice as did the troops of Napoleon.

There was, however, one point on which even the most dedicated scholars were dumbfounded. The translation of hieroglyphics still eluded them and thus the monuments of the ancients remained nameless and silent. The uncovering of a broken slab of black basalt by soldiers digging a trench at Rosetta near Alexandria in 1799 was to prove the key. However, it was not until 1822 that a frail young Frenchman named Jean François Champollion (1790–1832) detected a pattern in these enigmatic symbols. Starting with the names of Ptolemy and Cleopatra, Champollion gradually pieced together the archaic language of the pharaohs.

Then followed the great era of egyptology which coincided with the rise of European Imperialism. It was the age of Giovanni Belzoni (1778–1823), Sir Flinders Petrie (1853–1942), E. A. Wallis Budge (1857–1934), Gaston Maspero (1846–1916), and Howard Carter (1874–1939) among many others. Little by little the mysteries were revealed, the mummies and precious artefacts of the pharaohs were unearthed and shipped to Cairo, London, Paris or Berlin. But, as old mysteries were explained, new ones emerged to take their place.

The discovery of the tomb of the boy-king Tutankhamun in 1922 again brought egyptology into prominence. The extravagant contents of the small sepulchre captivated the entire world, influencing fashion and taste for generations to come. Of course the rash of sudden deaths which followed the discovery ensured the legendary status of the Valley of the Kings as belief in the Curse of the Pharaohs became common currency. Soon the sinister figure of the vengeful mummy lurched across cinema screens everywhere, an image that belied the true legacy of a complex and sophisticated culture.

The Land of the Nile

The Two Lands of Upper and Lower Egypt represented the long narrow ribbon of land following the course of the fertile river Nile, through raging cataracts, pitiless desert and finally to the lush green delta on the coast of the Mediterranean. It had been so since King Narmer united the two parts in pre-dynastic times, in around 3150 BC, although the very word 'Egypt' dates only from the period of Alexander the Great (332–323 BC). The word derives from the ancient name for the temple of Ptah at Memphis which was called the Haikuptah, corrupted by the Macedonian invaders into 'Aigyptos' and hence to our 'Egypt'. The people of the Nile's valley themselves had various names for their homeland including The Land of Khem which means 'the Black One', referring to the fertile soil which sustained them. Incidentally, the word 'Khem' has come down to us because of the magical reputation of the Egyptians. It is the root of the mystical art of alchemy and its more respectable scientific descendant chemistry.

The hard-working people of the Nile valley also referred to their land as Ta Neter meaning 'The Land of the Gods' and as Ta Meri, 'The Land of the Beloved'. Aside from this, the division between Upper and Lower Egypt led to more colourful descriptions. The lower component of the kingdom was known as The Red Land, symbolized by the Red Crown and the beautiful but deadly cobra-goddess Wadjet, while the Upper, more southerly portion of Pharaoh's dominion, was The White Land with a suitably hued crown to match, presided over by the vulture-goddess Nekhebet. It is because of this division, and the patronage of these two deities, that the ruler of Egypt was often described as He of the Two Ladies.

The Lower Land encompassed the swampy delta region of the Mediterranean coast and many of the sites featured in these chronicles. The capital of this area was Memphis, although the city of On, or Heliopolis as the Greeks called it, was also an important administrative and cult centre dedicated to the worship of the sun-god Ra. Within its borders are also found those vast and ancient inexplicable mysteries: the pyramids and the Great Sphinx of Giza. For centuries the Sphinx was known as the King of Terrors, because it was thought that the demons of the desert had sculpted it. It actually represents the power of the rising sun.

Upper Egypt was centred on the great city of Thebes, called by Homer Thebes of the Hundred Gates in contrast to the Greek Thebes, which had only seven. This was the site of the Great Temple of Karnak. The number and size of the gateways of this structure must have provided the inspiration for Homer's poetic description. Larger than any other religious edifice in the world, the Karnak Temple is dedicated to the worship of Amun-Ra, the supreme king of the gods, and it was also the home of the most powerful priestly faction in the Two Lands. The priests here provided the essential administrative skills necessary for the running of such a complex civilization. In Upper Egypt the ultimate reality was the desert. Here the pharaohs of the New

Kingdom secretly entombed their predecessors in a vast necropolis surrounded by barren limestone cliffs beyond the western shore of the Nile. Here we find the Valley of the Kings, the valleys of the Queens and Nobles, and the remains of vast mortuary temples and cyclopean memorials. The most notable of these is the beautiful temple built by the eccentric female pharaoh Hatshepsut (*d*. 1458 BC) at Deir el Bahri (see page 101), which commands the view from Luxor across the expanse of the Nile.

THE COMPANY OF GODS

In religious matters, the Ancient Egyptians were extremely conservative. Through conquest, foreign influence and invasion, new beliefs were absorbed even if they were incompatible with that which had gone before. The mythology therefore encompasses a vast array of gods, some universal and others peculiar to a single local-ity, many of whom were credited as the sole creators of the universe. Thus Amun, who had started as a minor patron deity of Thebes, eventually was identified with the all-powerful sun-god, Ra. He was considered the primal creator by many people in Upper Egypt, an act which he performed in the shape of a goose. Similarly, Geb the earth-god was known as the Great Cackler because of the noise he was rumoured to have made when laying the cosmic egg. Ptah, the artisan-god of Memphis, was said to have beaten out the sky on an anvil while, paradoxically, Nut the sky-goddess was thought to stretch from east to west above us in the form of the Celestial Cow, the stars being speckles on her belly. Neith, a goddess of hunting worshipped in the delta, was considered to be the mother of all the gods, having given birth to the sun, earth and heavens. The sun itself was at once thought to be the Boat of Millions of Years which conveyed Ra across the sky and also the right eye of Horus. The moon was the left eye of Horus but also the boat of Khonsu, son of Amun.

It has been suggested that the Ancient Egyptians were basically monotheistic, believing in a single god. The rationale behind this idea is that all their deities seem to be aspects or functions of the one primordial deity, Ra. The identity of this creator figure was disputed only once in Egypt's long history by the Eighteenth-Dynasty 'heretic', Pharaoh Amenophis IV, or Akhenaten (*d*. 1336 BC) who promoted exclusive worship of the Aten sun-disc (see page 48). The movement was short-lived as it was too much of a departure from established tradition.

The sun-god Ra was worshipped from earliest times under a bewildering variety of names and shapes. According to the priests of Heliopolis, Ra was born from a watery chaos called Nun. The first light emerged from a lotus which grew from a primeval mound, serenaded into existence by eight primordial frogs. This was Ra's first form, known as Atum. Finding that he had nowhere to stand, Atum-Ra created the dry earth and from him came all the other gods who are considered to be his descen-dants. Thus Ra is often called the first ancestor.

By an act of masturbation, Ra emitted the god Shu, or Air, and the goddess Tefnut, or Moisture. These in turn produced, Geb, the Earth, and Nut, the Sky. Forcibly separated from her lover by the will of Ra, Nut was not allowed to bear children on any day of the year, so the wise god Thoth played a game of dice with the moon and stole enough light from that orb to create five extra days, which is why the moon waxes and wanes. Upon each of these extra days a child was born to Nut. The first was the beneficent Osiris, the second, Horus the elder, and on the third day the dark and wilful Set was born. Lovely Isis came on the fourth while the fifth saw the emergence of gentle Nephthys. These gods are called the Company of Heliopolis. They, with the addition of the mummified figure of Ptah the Artisan, ibis-headed or baboon-shaped Thoth, the jackal-god Anubis the Embalmer, hawk-headed Horus the Avenger, and Maat, goddess of justice along with a host of minor deities, are the divine cast list of the chronicles.

Human beings and all other living things were created from the tears of Ra, although some held that they were fashioned upon a potter's wheel by ram-headed Khnum, who later set such a wheel in the womb of every female being so that he would not have to spend eternity populating the earth. When all things were accomplished and in their proper place, and all the creatures that were lived according to their natures and all the gods that maintained them were at their stations, Ra, the greatest and first of the deities, went to live among men as a mortal pharaoh.

Since Ra had been the first pharaoh, it naturally followed that all subsequent rulers partook of his divine nature. Thus all pharaohs were gods on earth and considered to be sons of Ra. Ancient Egyptian kings also took on the attributes of other gods, most prominently those of Horus the Younger, who was the son of Osiris and Isis. It would be fair to say that during his lifetime a king would be considered the Living Horus, while at death he would be identified with Osiris, lord of the underworld. Spells and magical formulae from The Book of the Coming Forth By Day (The Book of the Dead) were employed to ensure this transition.

THE MAGIC OF NAMES

Belief in magic was an integral part of Ancient Egyptian culture. It was believed that the essence of any person, animal, object or indeed of the gods themselves was contained within its true name. Ra, for instance, had many names but his real power resided in his hidden name which was engraved upon his heart at the moment of creation. The ancients were convinced that to possess the true name of Ra would make the possessor all-powerful. On a more mundane level, children were given two names, one for general use and the other to be jealously guarded for fear it might be used in malign enchantment. This belief in the power of names extended to funerary practices. In tomb paintings the gods are repeatedly begged to make the

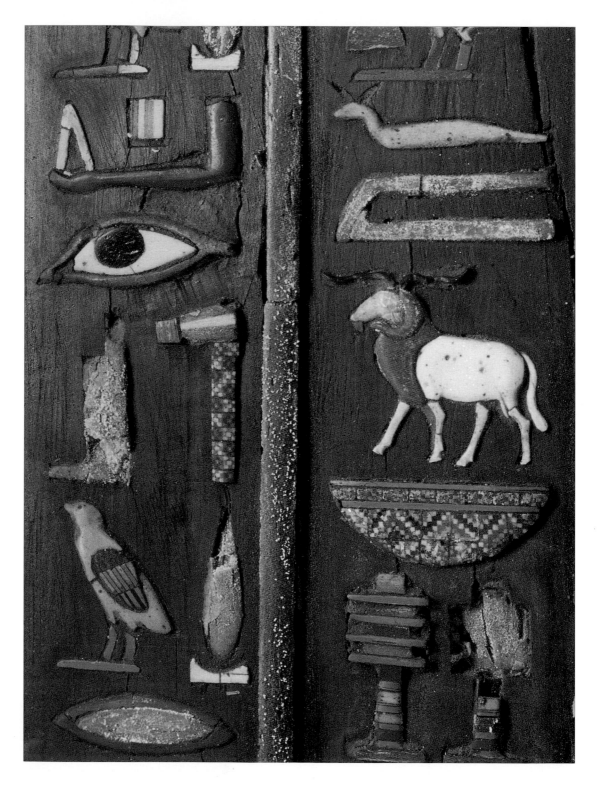

deceased's name live forever to ensure his or her immortality. This is the primary reason that the pharaohs of old were so keen to build enormous statues, temples and mortuary palaces eternally to enshrine their names. Conversely, disgraced rulers such as Hatshepsut (*d*. 1458 BC), Akhenaten (*d*. 1336 BC) and even Tutankhamun (*d*. 1325 BC) were condemned to oblivion by having their names systematically erased from monuments which were originally raised in their honour.

THE LEGACY OF THE SCRIBES

Scribes were vital to life in Ancient Egypt. The people regarded literacy so highly that they exhorted their sons to study in order to become scribes and escape labouring in the fields under the hot sun, or bearing a spear as a warrior. For scribes who had mastered the intricacies of hieroglyphic symbols and the simpler demotic script used in day-to-day affairs, anything was possible. As a skilful scribe one could achieve a rank and position impossible for one's brethren; in a grand temple perhaps, or even at the royal court. Given the prominence of these men and the prestige associated with their abilities it is not surprising that so much documentary evidence remains of life in the Two Lands over a period of 3,000 years. In addition to tax surveys, memorial inscriptions and personal letters, scribes also chronicled the memories and dreams of the people. Their amazing legacy, recorded on long strips of papyrus, reveals legends of long-dead pharaohs and powerful but enigmatic gods as well as the humbler tales of their own lives.

It is a sobering thought to realize that, as the author of this work, I am making the names 'live again' for a new generation; this is what an inhabitant of the Two Lands would have understood as the chronicles of Ancient Egypt. So now, let the tales of the people of the Two Lands speak for themselves.

Isis

My nod governs the shining heights of heaven,

The wholesome sea-breezes,

The lamentable depths below,

I am worshipped in many aspects,

Known by countless names,

Propitiated by all manner of different rites,

Yet the whole earth venerates Isis.

FROM *The Golden Ass* BY LUCIUS APULEIUS

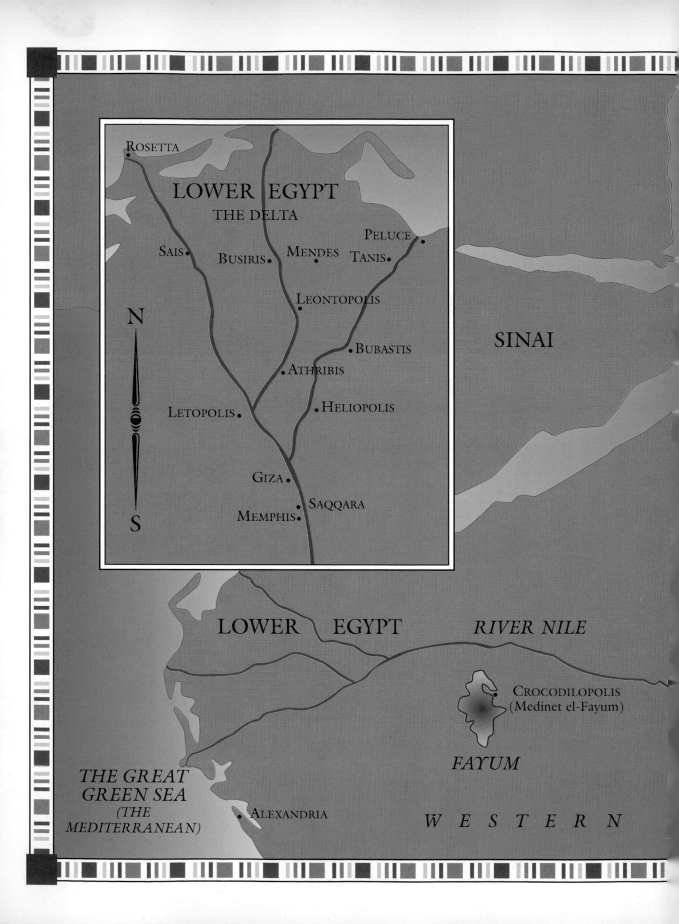

ROSETTA

LOWER EGYPT
THE DELTA

PELUCE

SAIS

BUSIRIS   MENDES   TANIS

LEONTOPOLIS

BUBASTIS

ATHRIBIS

LETOPOLIS   HELIOPOLIS

N

GIZA

SAQQARA

MEMPHIS

S

SINAI

LOWER   EGYPT   *RIVER NILE*

CROCODILOPOLIS
(Medinet el-Fayum)

FAYUM

*THE GREAT
GREEN SEA*
*(THE
MEDITERRANEAN)*   ALEXANDRIA   *W E S T E R N*

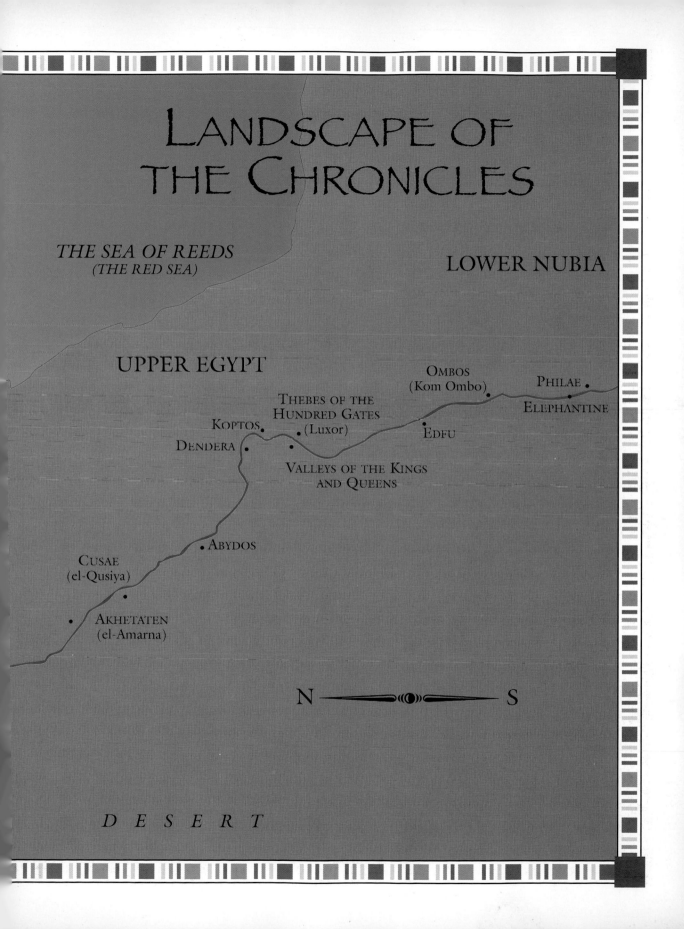

LANDSCAPE OF THE CHRONICLES

THE SEA OF REEDS
(THE RED SEA)

LOWER NUBIA

UPPER EGYPT

OMBOS
(Kom Ombo)

PHILAE

ELEPHANTINE

THEBES OF THE
HUNDRED GATES
(Luxor)

KOPTOS

DENDERA

EDFU

VALLEYS OF THE KINGS
AND QUEENS

ABYDOS

CUSAE
(el-Qusiya)

AKHETATEN
(el-Amarna)

N ——●—— S

D E S E R T

The Tales of the Gods

THE TALES OF THE GODS

THE VAST PANTHEON of Ancient Egyptian deities ranged from the universal forces of creation, such as the mighty Ra and his descendants, to smaller, more humble, local gods. Certain animals were regarded as the worldly manifestation of a particular god and were revered accordingly. There were also numerous fertility spirits and genii as well as the Kas of departed humans to honour and propitiate.

'The Eye of Ra' was a title bestowed on several goddesses who were daughters and descendants of the sun-god. The story here describes the vengeful Sekhmet, the personification of the fierce rays of the midday sun. The tale comes from hieroglyphics inscribed in a side chamber in the tomb of Pharaoh Seti I. It has been found nowhere else in the annals of Egyptian mythology. However, a fine statue of Sekhmet sits regally in her own sanctuary at Karnak.

'The Journey of Ra' is sculpted within the tomb of the pharaoh Seti I in the Valley of the Kings. Eleven hours only are given, fortunately the twelfth is frequently found in papyrus documents though, for some reason, it is rare in sculpture. The epic tale of the murder of the god-king Osiris, the tribulations of his devoted wife Isis and the struggles of his avenging son Horus has been pieced together from the writings of the Roman historian Plutarch. His work is likely to represent an accurate version of Osirian beliefs since he himself was a convert to the worship of Isis and her husband. Plutarch's writings take the form of an educational treatise addressed to a fellow convert, a lady called Klea, at Delphi in the second century AD. The cunning of Isis and her attempt to discover the hidden

name of Ra was found on a Twentieth-Dynasty papyrus. The story of Isis and the scorpions was sculpted on the back of a rounded stela which was found at Alexandria at the start of the nineteenth century. It forms one of a class of stelae usually known as 'Cippi of Horus' on which numerous spells to ward off ill-fortune and venomous animals are inscribed.

The accounts of the court of the gods are taken from a well-preserved papyrus scroll, now in the Chester Beatty Library, Dublin. The less than respectful way in which the gods are dealt with in this text is unusual. Many of the deities seem prone to doubt and spite and, as a result, this story is more reminiscent of the mythology of Greece rather than that of Ancient Egypt.

The episode of the black pig comes from the Ancient Egyptian Book of the Dead. This was a collection of spells and incantations to accompany the deceased on the journey to the other world and to ensure that he or she passed safely through the Gates of Night into the presence of Osiris. These must have been so numerous and well known that they were rarely written down and hence have not survived.

The final climactic battles of Horus are sculpted in great detail on the great Temple of Horus at Edfu. The present form of the temple was begun in the reign of Ptolemy III Euergetes I, a pharaoh of Macedonian origins and ancestor of the celebrated Cleopatra. It took over 180 years to build and decorate, probably being completed about 100 BC. It is likely that the temple was the setting for some form of mystery play in which the Pharaoh or his representative would take on the role of Horus.

THE EYE OF RA

NOW RA, THE GREATEST OF the gods, reigned on earth as a mortal pharaoh in the midst of humanity, who had sprung from his tears, and surrounded by his family who were all known as the Company of Heliopolis. And among these numbered Osiris, who was the sun-god's heir; his sister-wife Isis; Horus the Elder, who so resembled Ra that he was called his son; Set the wily; and his sister-wife Nephthys the dark.

All these, though they had the guise of mortals, lived far longer than any human being. However, no one was sad, for the prosperity that flowed from the power of the divine King ensured that happiness reigned upon the earth. None starved; for the harvests were so bounteous that the people later spoke fondly of all the good things that occurred in the time of Ra.

But the nature of humanity is such that they forget. After a period of three hundred and sixty years the great god, still guised as a mortal man, grew old. And in his age he showed the signs of infirmity. He dribbled and muttered to himself as his eyes grew dimmer and he grew ever more insular and forgetful.

Men no longer gave him the respect that is due to a king and god, but mocked him saying: 'Look upon Ra, he is old, his bones are as soft as silver, his flesh is as soft as gold and his hair brittle like lapis lazuli.' But Ra did not hear them, for in his old age he had grown deaf.

Now the goddess Isis supported Ra in his infirmity and when his spittle fell upon the ground she took it up and kept it, though not even she yet knew the reason and nor would she until her husband was dead. But more will be told of this.

The other gods of the Company of Heliopolis were much disturbed by the laughter of men for the awe of the gods had gone and Ra had become a buffoon. It was even suggested by Set that one of them should replace him upon the throne of the world, but Osiris the Good was loyal to his ancestor and would not countenance such treachery. So nought came of it and Ra went on as before. In vain did Osiris and his brothers and sisters plead with Ra to renew the fertility of the earth; but no sooner had they spoken than Ra had forgotten their words.

Thus did the earth ail and men and women, laughing no longer, cried out against Ra and the gods and rose in rebellion in the Northern Land and the Southern Land. Soon the temples were thrown down and the images of the Company of Heliopolis lay shattered in the dust. No longer were plentiful offerings made to the gods, for the prayers of the hungry went unanswered. All too soon prayers turned to curses and the name of Ra was vilified upon the lips of men.

Now, at last, Ra bestirred himself for he had lost all of his earthly kingdom. His mortal power was gone and he bemoaned his foolishness. Calling together his kin Ra sought their advice too late, for none could advise him. So he took himself to the great swamp where life had first begun and there pleaded for the counsel of Nun, his primordial parent who manifested himself in the shape of a green man streaming with water and weeds, the sacred lotus upon his godly brow.

'O eldest of the gods, first ancestor,' began Ra, 'in my foolishness I have taken the form and nature of a mortal man and entered time to live amongst humanity who were born of my tears. But now these ingrates have turned against me and my descendants. They overthrow the temples and curse my name. What should I do?'

The deep voice of Nun rang forth. 'My son who named me and gave me form, mightiest of gods, greatest of kings, your throne is safe though it seems about to fall. Return to Heliopolis and there pluck out your eye and send it forth against those who would attack you.' So saying, the ancient god sank back into the primeval waters.

Then did Ra return to the City of the Sun and, there enthroned, gouged out his eye. Terrible was his pain, horrifying were his cries, and dreadful was his towering rage. All these fierce passions found form as his eye found shape as a fearsome lioness with teeth and claws that ached to rend flesh.

Heedless of the blood that coursed down his cheek, Ra called out: 'Sekhmet the mighty do I name you, and Nesert who is a burning flame.' Thus was his new-born daughter given a measure of the sun-god's immortal power.

Then the terrible roar of Sekhmet sounded forth: 'Flee from me O humanity, though it shall avail you not. Hide in the deserts and the mountains, let fear grow in your hearts; for I am vengeance and bloody death.'

Then the powerful lioness went out into the Two Lands of Egypt and everywhere she met with men she slew them. Armies were formed and brought against her but these were easily defeated with not one man left alive to survey the carnage of Sekhmet's ferocious passion.

Day after day the lioness Sekhmet charged into the fray. None could resist her might as she rent the very flesh from the bones of men, greedily lapping up their blood until she was gorged to bursting. As she progressed down the Nile valley as far as Henen-seten she slew where she could, even though humanity fought no more but fled her terrible wrath. Each night she returned to the palace of Ra and boasted of her victories: 'This day I have been mighty amongst mankind. Not one stands alive where I have been. I have waded in human blood and drunk my fill for the joy of killing gladdens my heart.'

The company of gods was not glad for now that men were scattered there were none to make the offerings in the temples. Osiris and Shu, who were always the champions of humanity, pleaded with Ra to end the slaughter.

'First Father Ra,' they began. 'Surely you have reaped sufficient vengeance for the laughter and mockery of men. Let your daughter rest now lest she destroy all that you have created.'

Ra was silent for a long while before he replied. 'As always, wise Osiris and com-passionate Shu have spoken the truth. I, too, have sickened of this blood-thirst and would have no more of it. When next my daughter Sekhmet comes before me I will command her to cease.' Hearing these words, Osiris and Shu were content.

That night Sekhmet, gory with the marks of her combat, returned to Heliopolis. Presenting herself before her father Ra, she recounted the number of the dead, her prowess in battle and of how it pleased her to slay so many. But Ra was grave.

'My daughter, I created you from my rage and pain, but these have now passed and I repent of my rashness. Slay no more but settle here with me. Allow mankind to multiply once more and they will honour you as a goddess.'

'Great Father, can it be that you are not so great as I had supposed?' replied Sekhmet, her mighty jaws gaping with astonishment. 'Does your courage fail you now that absolute victory is in sight? Do the weak counsels of lesser gods sway your judgement? If that is so then it is time that you stepped down from your throne and allowed another, stronger deity to rule.'

'Can it be you who harbours such ambition?' demanded Ra.

'No Father, for it is my delight to drink the blood of my enemies. It is I who see the rightness of my actions even if you do not. For destruction did you create me, and thus will I destroy. Your weak and feeble will cannot halt me for it was for this that I was made.' So saying, Sekhmet left the palace roaring: 'Flee from me O humanity, though it shall avail you not; for I am Sekhmet, I am vengeance and bloody death.'

So it was that Sekhmet continued her bloody progress and rejoiced in her blood-thirst. Ra was greatly disturbed by his daughter's words and quickly summoned the company of the gods of Heliopolis to advise him. One by one they came forward, but none had any advice to offer. The full horror of his mistake now dawned upon Ra.

'Then if none of the gods can help me to end this monster's reign I must beg humanity to aid me,' he thought. 'It is my daughter who causes this carnage therefore it is to the daughters of men that I will turn.'

Ra then sent the Company of Heliopolis out into the world to seek the survivors of Sekhmet's wrath. So the gods went forth and their speed was like that of a storm wind. Soon many men and women were gathered in the holy city of Heliopolis while outside the walls Sekhmet murdered their kin. Ra spoke again to the company of gods: 'Go now far to the south to Elephantine, the first cataract of the bloodied Nile. There procure the mandrake plants and bring them back to me.'

Again the gods went out and with the furious speed of the desert wind returned to their ancestor with the precious scarlet herbs. Then Ra commanded that the daughters of men brew beer. So they set to work and crushed many bushels of barley and soon seven thousand jugs of beer were ready. To each of the seven thousand jugs Ra added a potion made from the mandrake plant. At once the mixture

THE OPET FESTIVAL

ON FIRST impression, Ancient Egyptian society may appear morbid, centring on mummification and the afterlife, but nothing could be further from the truth. The inhabitants of the Two Lands viewed the celebration of life as complementary to the ritual of death. The Opet, or Heavenly, Festival in particular, was a spectacular excuse to loosen the bonds of propriety.

The festival occurred in the second month of the season of Akhet, or July by our reckoning, and lasted from two to four weeks. It coincided with the helical rising of the exceptionally bright star Sirius, or Sothis as the Egyptians knew it, identified with the goddess Isis. This, in turn, marked the annual flooding of the Nile which was vital for agriculture and survival. It was also believed to represent the fathering of the Pharaoh by the mighty Amun-Ra himself.

From the Great Temple of Karnak the processional boat of the god Amun would be brought out bearing his image. Likewise a boat was carried from the nearby temple of Mut the Mother. When the two met on the avenue of the ram-headed sphinxes it signalled rejoicing, drunkenness and wild abandon as temple offerings were redistributed among the people.

At the climax of the festival the King entered the dark and shrouded inner sanctum of Amun where mysterious rites enabled him to take on aspects of eternity before returning to his people as a living god.

took on a scarlet hue. Then pomegranate juice was added, making the beer look even more sanguine. The final addition was a small amount of human blood, of which there was no shortage. Now the beer of Heliopolis had all the appearance of that which runs in man's veins.

Before light flooded the sky Ra commanded that the seven thousand jugs be placed before the city so that Sekhmet would come upon them first. Some say that the ruby contents were poured over the land so that it had the appearance of a sea of blood. This was the scene that Sekhmet saw when she arrived at Heliopolis. She was entranced by her beautiful reflection in the ensanguined liquid. Admiring her loveliness for a while, she then smelt the heady aroma and bent her head to lap up the brew. So delicious did she find it that soon she had consumed it all, and then fell drunkenly to the ground. The gods and frightened men emerged from the city and cautiously approached the snoring lioness. Then Ra put forth his power once more and drew from Sekhmet a portion of her terrible strength and, just as she had come from him, he created a new being with her nature but without her hatred. Some say this was the cat-goddess Bast, though others claim that it was as the gentle, fun-loving cow-goddess Hathor that this part of Sekhmet found new form.

The lioness Sekhmet awoke to find her rage and blood-lust gone. Though still a goddess of vengeance she was more gentle and protective henceforth. She married the god Ptah and went to reside at Memphis where she was known as the Lady in the Blood-stained Robe.

Ra, for his part, was sickened by the madness which earthly life had inflicted upon him, so he chose to abandon the mortal world for evermore and dwell in his celestial realm within the sun-boat that is called Manzet in the morning and Mesektet at dusk. But to this day at the Festival of the New Year beer is brewed in jugs, one each for every priestess of Ra. This is consumed with much merriment, for by this brew mankind was once saved from the fury of a goddess.

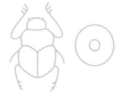

THE JOURNEY OF RA

WHEN THE MIGHTY RA CREATED the world, two rivers came into being. The first of these is the sacred Nile itself, born in the two caverns of the far south which are under the rulership of ram-headed Khnum, lord of the source of life. The river itself is the god Hapi from whom the prosperity of the Two Lands flows. The second river exists both in the sky and under the earth and it is upon this river that the barque, which is called Manzet in the morning and Mesektet at dusk, sails.

In the daytime, the great god Ra voyages in this barque through the sky in such glory that it is madness to stare upon him. Within his Boat of Millions of Years are Weneb his scribe who sets down everything the god sees, Maat the goddess of justice, Thoth the lord of wisdom, and bright Horus who acts as steersman. Two fish called Abtu and Ant accompany the boat to ensure that nothing obstructs its heavenly course.

At noon Ra can see both the farthest west and the farthest east. He observes the mountains called Manu and Bakhu; for just as Manu occupies the west, its twin Bakhu lies in the east. Vast and awesome are these two, and so high that the very sky rests upon their summits. On the topmost peak of Bakhu dwells a huge serpent thirty cubits in length. His scales are made of flint and strong metal. He guards the mountain and the Great Green Sea, and none may pass him save the boat of Ra which is called Manzet in the morning.

Each evening the Mesektet boat eases itself into the western sky approaching the mountain called Manu where lies the first of the Gates of Night, entrance to the Land of the Dead. As the boat passes, a lament rises from the sacred apes of the mountain, for Ra the glorious is dead. At the opening, a company of gods mournfully awaits the Mesektet boat. Even on this sad occasion they cannot but marvel at its trappings: the jasper, gold and emeralds which have gone into its making, the turquoise, lapis lazuli and amethyst which bedeck its prow and stern.

Now the gods take up towing ropes and pull the resplendent vessel along the river. The portals of the other world are flung wide and the twelve goddesses of night board the barque to guide it through the dismal gloom of this terrible place. Each goddess is an experienced navigator and, without them, not even the body of Ra would be able to pass safely through the twelve kingdoms of darkness, for the foul serpent Apep lies in wait to devour the sun-god. The first kingdom of night is called the Watercourse of Ra. This land is sombre, yet not completely without light for on each side of the river are six serpents, coiled and erect, who eternally breathe illuminating fire. At this hour, Ra lies within his cabin, cold and lifeless. At the prow stands wolf-headed Upauat, the opener of the ways, and the goddess Sa the protectress who is the first of the goddesses of night. These two stand in the way of any peril that may befall their lord and ancestor Ra. Thus passes the first hour of the night, and the second hour is at hand.

At the entrance to the second kingdom is a huge gate. Tall are the walls which surround it and narrow the passageway through which the river flows. Sharp spearheads are set about the walls so that none may climb over and a vicious snake stands guardian. None may pass under this serpent save those who know his name. But this is not the end of the dangers for, within the narrow pass, two further serpents are to be found, one above and one lurking in the waters below. Their breath is of fire mingled with poison so that the very air is tainted with their venom. Now does Sa, goddess of the first hour, give way to the goddess of the second who calls aloud the name of the great serpent. At these words the gate is flung wide and the fire and poison cease. Thus does the boat of Ra come safely through the pass and enter the country called Ur-nes, where dwell the souls of kings and Ra is undoubted lord. Those who live here are at peace and happy for this is also the land where the merry god Bes makes his home, and with him are Nepra and Tepu-yn, the spirits of fertility and wheat. Thus passes the second hour of the night.

Now the third hour is at hand and the third goddess of the night takes her place at the prow. She calls out to the serpent-guardian of the third gate, and the boat of Ra passes safely through. Watercourse of the Only God is the name of this realm for this is the kingdom of Osiris, he who is overlord of the entire Land of the Dead. Enthroned is Osiris, surrounded by the gods who pay him homage. Mummified to the neck, Osiris holds the Crook and Flail of sovereignty and carries upon his head the White Crown of the Southern Land. Great is Osiris, for all who die must come before him for judgement: when the heart of man is set on one side of a balance with the feather of Maat on the other. His throne stands in the midst of a stream and from the waters rises a single lotus blossom, the colour of the morning sky. Upon its petals stand the four sons of Horus who assist Osiris in the judgement and who protect the organs of the dead. They are the human-headed Imsety, who rules the south and is protector of the liver; the ape-headed Hapy who rules the north, and is protector of

26

the lungs; jackal-headed Duamutef, governor of the east, protector of the stomach; and Qebehsenuef, lord of the west, who protects the intestines.

This third hour is the hour that the evil man fears; for by his own actions is he condemned as his heart sinks lower and lower until it provides food for the monster Amemt the Devourer. Then is the soul of the evil man cast out to dwell with the abominable serpent Apep and to fall at last into the everlasting pits of fire. But those who have lived in the just ways of Maat, who have hurt no one by fraud or violence, who have helped the widow and the orphan, who have clothed the shipwrecked mariner, who have given food to the hungry and charity to the crippled, who have not caused the shedding of tears nor stirred up strife: for these souls the heart rises up to the hand of Thoth the wise, who places it again within the breast of the man and leads him to the fertile field of reeds where he may dwell in happiness for evermore. Thus passes the third hour of the night and the goddess of the fourth hour takes her place in the prow, calling the name of the guardian of the fourth realm.

The fourth realm is called Living One of Forms and is also the dominion of Osiris. Dismal is this realm; a wasteland of sand, limitless and gloomy. Nothing grows or prospers save the hordes of many-headed serpents who hiss and roar. Some of these

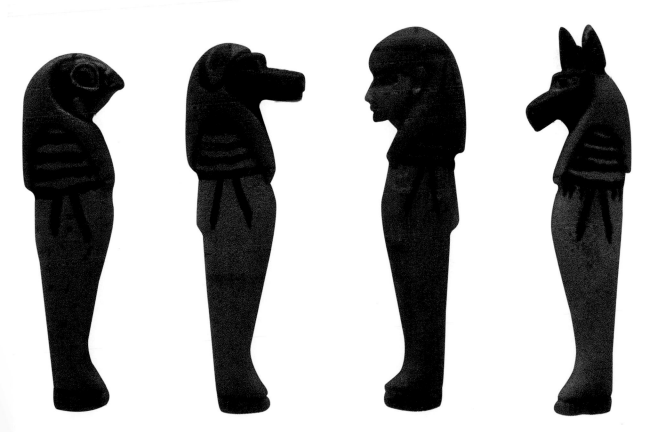

serpents crawl upon the ground but others spread vast wings to take to the air. Still others walk upon legs like a man's. Angry are these creatures but their anger is not directed at the boat of Ra, so again the dead god safely passes through.

The landscape is changed, for here the river is no more. Where it lay is now a deep ravine; its walls of rock rise steeply and the wind never ceases to howl. This place is called The Mouth of the Tomb. At the urging of the fourth goddess, the sacred boat becomes a beautiful glittering snake which bears Ra and the gods upon its back. The serpent's eyes are watchful for always the dark Apep is a danger so it glides across the sand with its fangs extended in readiness. Thus passes the fourth hour of the night.

Again the goddesses change places as the fifth realm is breached. This chasmed kingdom is called Hidden and is ruled by Seker, who has the form of a mummified falcon. He dwells beneath a high mound of sand. On either side are two guardian sphinxes with the faces of men and outstretched claws to seize the intruder. On the mound lies a three-headed snake with outstretched wings and, between them, stands Seker himself, come to pay homage to Ra. Seker is given the task of punishing rebels by plunging them into a boiling lake. These unfortunates now repent and cry out to Ra to save them, but Ra is dead and hears them not as his boat passes on its way.

On the other wall of the great chasm is the home of Night and Darkness. Here the scarab, Khepera, waits for he is the soul of the universe. Seeing the boat approach

Khepera takes wing to land upon the recumbent body of the dead Ra. Poised now to return to Ra his life, Khepera is content to wait and let the night progress. Now there falls a gleam of light, for the Morning Star stands by the next gate and it is truly said that in the darkest night there is a promise of the coming day. Thus passes the fifth hour of the night.

The realm of the sixth hour is called the Abyss of the Waters. Ruled by Osiris, he is here worshipped as the lord of fertility who brings forth green things upon the earth. Now the boat of Ra is again upon the river and all the gods rejoice, for the hours of the night are passing away. On the banks of the river are the mysterious shapes of unnamed gods who bow before the boat of Ra. Nine sceptres stand proudly there each also proclaiming the right of one of the company of gods. Now a huge lion is seen and three shrines, the meaning of which is not meant for men to know. Khepera stirs from his place of rest upon the bosom of Ra and flies to a five-headed serpent to lie within its coils, for this marks the half-way point of night and further lies the way to sunrise. Thus passes the sixth hour of the night.

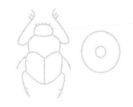

The goddess of the seventh hour opens wide the gates to the realm called the Secret Cavern, for this is the place of awesome peril. It is here that the abominable monster Apep makes his fetid home. In the midst of the river is a sand-bank which is four hundred and fifty cubits long, but the coils of Apep cover it so completely that nothing of it can be seen. His roars can chill the bones and freeze the blood in a man's veins as they thunder throughout the Land of the Dead. Now he comes, his terrible jaws wide-stretched to swallow the boat of Ra, but he will not be victorious for in the prow stands Isis, she of the many names, goddess of magic, whose enchantments none can resist. As the ravenous creature rears above her Isis does not falter but raises her hands and speaks the words of imperishable power. By her will the great cobra Mehen rises from the waters and opens his hood to shield the dead god Ra from the evil of Apep. All the while Isis chants her spells and casts a curse of binding upon the monster. Then the goddesses Selket, the scorpion, and Herdesuf leap down to the sand-bank where they strike him with knives and spears, weakening him so that he can be bound fast with the spells of Isis. These two remain behind as the boat of Ra passes in safety, yet Apep does not die for the monster is immortal and every night will he lie in wait to attack the boat of Ra. Thus passes the seventh hour of the night, moving now from darkness towards sunrise.

Now the boat passes into the eighth realm which is called Sarcophagus of the Gods. Here dwell the souls of dead gods who call to Ra, but so far away are they that the sound they make is like the bellowing of bulls, the cries of birds, the wail of mourners and the murmurings of bees. The boat is escorted by the Nine Followers of the Gods. Before it are the four souls representing the primordial earth-god Tatanen in the form of fierce rams. The first is crowned with upstanding plumes, the second with the Red Crown of the North, the third with the White Crown of the South, the fourth with the shining disc of the sun. These four are worshipped at Memphis for in this land Ptah is ruler and they are but shadows of that god.

Now the ninth hour is come and the boat enters the realm called Procession of Images. Full and strong the river runs now and the boat is borne forward on its stream. Twelve star-gods hold paddles to aid the course of the boat in case of need. The star-gods sing now to praise Ra and urge him to live again. No darkness broods here, for this is the place where the dead receive the offerings made to them on earth.

Abyss of Waters, Lofty of Banks is the name of the tenth hour of the night; a friendly land whose dwellers come down to the shore to greet the passing of the sun. The current is rushing, bearing Ra and his attendants swiftly forward. Four goddesses now cast beams of light to dispel the darkness. Before the boat races the

MAAT

THE CONCEPT OF Maat was central to Ancient Egyptian thought. Often simply translated as justice, Maat actually expresses the proper order of the universe, right thinking, correct action and the regulation of time and space. It has hints of social propriety, the pyramidical nature of interaction between people, the respect that is due to a father, the duties one should show to a son. It encompassed the majesty of the Pharaoh and the loyalty that is owed to him by a subject, as well as his duty to protect and nurture his people. There is no doubt that pharaohs believed that they ruled under the auspices of Maat.

Maat was personified as a goddess from earliest times. A daughter of Ra, Maat came into existence as the cosmos was born. She can be thought of as a female equivalent to wise Thoth; like him, a regulator of the seasons who keeps the stars in their proper courses. She is usually portrayed wearing an ostrich feather on her head, or simply as the feather itself. It is in this form that she is central to the judgement of the dead. It is she who is set in the balance against the heart of the deceased to measure whether he was 'justified' in life or not. The place of judgement in the underworld, where Osiris sits, is known as the Hall of Maat.

Though there are few temples to Maat she was widely honoured, so much so that the chief minister of the Pharaoh was given the title High Priest of Maat.

Morning Star in the form of a crowned double-headed serpent upon human legs. Leader of Heaven is his name. This is the greatest of all the kingdoms of night for it is here the wondrous miracle takes place, for Khepera rejoins Ra and merges with him so that the two are now one. Thus does Ra, he who has been dead for so long, weakly return to life.

Onward goes the boat of heaven, onward to sunrise and new light. Thus passes the tenth hour. Now the eleventh hour has come. This is called the Mouth of the Cavern, where the river has fallen and is sluggish so the boat is drawn onward and upward by the gods who tow it with the body of the cobra Mehen, who is Ra's protector, serving as a rope. A red star set in the prow casts a lurid glow over this land. Here are the terrible pits of fire which are the final destination of the wicked. Goddesses, whose form is horrifying and whose breath is flame, guard the pits and torment the damned souls while Horus watches to ensure that the sentence of his father Osiris is carried out. No help can come to these unfortunates, no escape is possible for they are doomed by their own actions on earth. On the other side of the river stands the stellar spirit Shadu, he who is recognized by the three stars which make up his belt. Thus passes the eleventh hour.

Now is the twelfth hour. Dawn is at hand and the goddesses of the hours call out the name of this new land: it is called Darkness Has Fallen and Births Shine Forth. Khepera mounts the prow for he has taken on the essence of Ra and he is the sun in the morning. Now he is ready to complete the transformations of Ra before the boat leaves the underworld. This land is unlike any other, because it lies within the body of a vast serpent whose name is Life of the Gods. Now the Boat of Millions of Years traverses the beast's gut and Ra becomes Khepera, full of strength as he stands upon the prow. Twelve goddesses wait at the serpent's mouth to seize the tow ropes and draw the boat to the eastern horizon near Mount Bakhu. The corpse of the old Ra is cast from the boat, for the old Ra is made anew and the world is filled with light. Thus are the transformations of the sun-god completed and his boat, which is called Manzet in the morning, progresses through the twelve kingdoms of the day, all of which are ruled by Ra.

OSIRIS AND ISIS

FTER RA, FIRST ANCESTOR and sun-god, had departed from the earth, the throne of the world was bestowed on Osiris who reigned thereafter as a mortal pharaoh in the place of Ra. And with him were his sister-wife Isis and his brothers Horus the Elder and Set, with Set's sister-wife Nephthys.

It has already been told of how the curse of Ra was upon their mother Nut, and how the god Thoth tricked the moon into giving enough light to create five extra days upon which each of these five gods could be born. Osiris was the eldest son and his birth had been marked with wonders and prodigies for a mighty voice was heard in all the earth crying: 'The Lord of all comes forth into the light.' And a woman drawing water at the well of the temple of Heliopolis was so stricken by the divine power that she prophesied saying: 'Osiris the King is born, he who will save the world.'

Now, when Osiris was grown and come to the throne, the Two Lands were in a tragic state. Ever since the terrible days of Sekhmet the lioness barbarism had ruled; for men, once having been taught warfare, battled against each other and feasted upon human flesh. They had forgotten the kindly ways of the ancient gods and the just ways of Maat. Lawlessness was supreme and savagery rife.

However, when Osiris became Pharaoh he walked amongst his people without fear and taught them to till the land and propagate vines. Osiris showed men how to pick fruit from trees and when Isis discovered barley and wild wheat, the good King revealed the right times to plant and reap crops. He forbade the consumption of human meat and instead encouraged the propagation of beasts. Osiris spoke of the Maat and educated all in the right way to honour the gods. Everywhere he went he made good laws and banished barbarism from the land. Great was the love and gratitude shown to Osiris, and for these acts he is known as Osiris the Benefactor.

But the safety and prosperity of the Two Lands was not enough for this kindly monarch, for the rest of the world suffered under the yoke of savagery also. So, with the regretful farewells of his subjects ringing in his ears, Osiris departed from the land of the Nile to bring his gifts to all others who dwelt under the light of Ra.

During the absence of Osiris, his loving wife Isis ruled in his stead but he was gone for so long that their deceitful brother Set cast covetous eyes upon the throne, longing for the power that belonged to Osiris. Now Set was wily and knew that it would do no good to make his claim publicly or to seize his desire, for none of the other gods would support him. With whispers and rumour he sought instead to undo the good works of his kingly brother and persuade all that it would be better for them if

Set was Pharaoh. Soon Set had gathered no less than seventy-two nobles of the realm to his cause, most prominent amongst them was the sly and subtle Queen Aso of Ethiopia whose mortal cunning was a match for Set's unnatural malice.

Set laid his web of lies with care during his brother's long absence so that none, not even Isis or his wife Nephthys, knew of Set's dark intent. However, Nephthys, though innocent of Set's evil, grew discontented for he spent long periods in the company of Queen Aso and neglected his duties as a husband.

So it was that in the twenty-eighth year of the reign of Osiris that news arrived of the long-departed King's return to Egypt. The people were overjoyed and even Set was pleased, though his reasons for happiness were contrary to those of all the people of the Two Lands.

Great was the celebration when the triumphant Pharaoh Osiris once again came to the Palace of Heliopolis. Trumpets sounded and banners flew to demonstrate the love and loyalty of the people and the happiness of Queen Isis. None seemed more happy than Set and Nephthys, though each had their own reasons for wishing to see their elder brother again. At the banquet that night each plied Osiris with beer and regaled him with tales so that when the time came for the Pharaoh to seek his bed he was befuddled with drink. Later, as Khonsu the moon sailed the sky, Nephthys garlanded herself with sweet-smelling flowers and dressed in the clothes of her sister Isis. She then secretly made her way to Osiris's bedchamber and lay down with him.

'My husband Set is barren and cannot give me a son,' she whispered, 'but you Osiris the Good, lord of fertility will fill my womb with seed and plough this furrow.' With these words she drew Osiris upon her and they were one. Little did she know that Set already lurked there in the darkness and witnessed his wife's infidelity and heard her insulting words. His hatred of Osiris, great before, now grew greater still.

As silently as she had come, Nephthys fled from the room. Set emerged from his hiding place and, taking out a length of cord, moved to his brother's prone form and carefully measured him in every part. Then he, too, departed cursing the name of Osiris in his heart.

With the aid of his seventy-two conspirators, Set had

35

a coffer made out of costly wood, painted and decorated with rich designs in vibrant colours. The workmanship of this box was so fine that all who saw it longed to possess it. But this was not its purpose for Set had used every measurement taken from Osiris's body in the construction of the box for it was here that the dark god intended that his brother should eternally lie.

Time passed and as the box grew ever more opulent, Nephthys blossomed too as she grew great with child. She believed that only she knew the identity of the true father of her baby, little realizing that her husband Set was privy to her secret too.

At length a child was born to Nephthys and he was given the name of Anubis. In celebration, Set, the reputed father, held a spectacular feast at his city of Tanis to which all the earthly gods and the most prominent of mortals were invited. Tales were told, boasts exchanged, dances performed and much beer was consumed. At the height of the banquet, the wily Set proposed a game.

'There has recently come into my possession,' began Set, 'a marvellous chest, the like of which I have never before seen.' At this a gorgeously decorated coffer was brought into the hall by two confederates of the cunning god. 'This box was brought from far Ethiopia by the will of that land's beautiful queen.' Set inclined his head towards the place of Aso, who returned his bow with her own.

'It is fitting on this night of rejoicing that this glorious object be offered as a prize to any that can fit within it, for the birth of a man's first son should be marked with unstinting generosity.' A ripple of applause went around the company as the box was placed in the centre of the room. 'Now my lords, and by the leave of King Osiris, who will be first to enter this most excellent of prizes?'

At once a nobleman leapt to his feet. 'I will be the first to try the test,' he cried and with no further delay he lay down in the coffer. Laughing, Set declared that the man was too short to win the game. Another attempted the test and then another but each one had some imperfection or other. One was too tall, one too fat, another too broad about the hips. One was too old and bent, yet another too wide about the shoulders and so it went on until each and every man and god around the room had attempted the box.

It was then that Set declared, 'Surely it is evident that the only one who can fit this wondrous object must be that one who is so perfect in every other way.' He turned to the throne and bowed before his brother Osiris. 'Tell me, my brother, great Osiris will you lie here before us all and prove your superiority?'

Smiling, Osiris rose to his feet and was about to reply when Isis swiftly whispered, 'Do not do it my lord, for Set is not to be trusted.'

Osiris kissed her softly replying, 'Do not be so foolish my love, it is only a harmless game.' So saying he stepped down from the throne, removed his crown and allowed Set to help him get into the box. As he lay there it was evident to all that he fitted it perfectly. He was neither too short or too tall, he was not too fat or thin.

'See how perfect is my brother Osiris,' cried Set. 'So wonderfully does he fit this coffer that it would be a shame if ever he left it.' Snarling with hate Set slammed down the heavy lid trapping Osiris within. The assembled company surged forward to save their king but they were too late for now Set's seventy-two confederates drew their swords to prevent interference. At a signal from Set a crucible of molten lead was brought and, with it, the malicious god sealed the box. With more than mortal strength Set then lifted it and bore it the banks of the Nile. 'Farewell my oh so perfect brother,' he gloated as he cast the chest into the swift-flowing waters.

Returning to the hall, Set laughed as he took up the discarded crown of Osiris and placed it upon his own head. 'The Two Lands may now hail their new king,' he exulted as the weeping Isis tore at her hair in grief and fled into the starlit night.

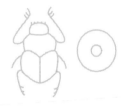

Wailing to the four winds, Isis, dishevelled and dirty, stumbled through the delta swamps. Her arms were scored with bloody welts, her eyes blinded with unquenchable tears as she mourned the terrible death of her beloved husband. In her insanity she conceived a plan so bold that no one who was sane would have dared contemplate it. She wandered far and wide asking each and every person that she met whether they had seen a large and ornate box float down the river. Each man and woman so approached was fearful of this bedraggled spectre so they answered that they had not and then hurried on their way.

And so it went on. The seasons passed according to the will of Ra. Set was content on the throne of the Two Lands and the people laboured beneath his tyranny. They, like Isis, wept for they too remembered the goodness of the dead Osiris. Nephthys also was sad, for not only did she mourn Osiris but she had been put aside by her vainglorious husband Set, just as he had disowned her infant son Anubis.

One day, while Isis sat moaning and rocking herself in the mud of the Nile, she heard some children talking. Her mad eyes widened as she heard them speak of a box they had seen floating upon the waters of the Great Green Sea. Leaping to her feet Isis swore that henceforth children would be granted the gift of prophecy. She then made all haste northwards for now she knew that to seek Osiris in Egypt would be in vain and that his corpse lay far away in the lands of the Asiatics.

Now the fate of the ornate coffer was this. After Set had cast the chest into the Nile, the flood had borne it northwards through the delta and out into the Great Green Sea. Buffeted by the waves for many months, it had finally come to rest in a tamarisk bush on the shores of distant Byblos. The bush, now empowered by its proximity to the corpse of a god, instantly put forth shoots and grew into a fine tree. Within the trunk of this mighty wonder lay the body of Osiris completely obscured from view. One day Melkart, the King of Byblos passed this place and noticing the strength and straightness of the tamarisk tree commanded that it be immediately felled to make a central pillar for his palace. So was it done, and so true was the trunk of the tree that the carpenters had only to trim off the side branches for it to fit its purpose to perfection. Thus it was that the revels of the court of Byblos took place about the body of Osiris all unknowing.

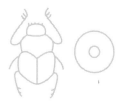

Some years later, there came to the city of Byblos a dirty and dishevelled woman who wept and tore her hair with grief. Her journey had been long and her disappointment terrible to behold as she rested by a well. It was this tearful vision that greeted the servants of the palace as they came to fetch water. The maids were so sorry for the madwoman that they brought her food and tried to assuage her weeping. Soon, she grew to trust them, to encourage them to speak of their lives and to dress their hair. This last she did most deftly breathing upon each strand so that a divine perfume surrounded each girl. When next they came before their queen, she was entranced by the beautiful odour that emanated from the maids. On being told of the sad woman by the well, the Queen summoned her to the palace.

The Queen and the beggar recognized each other as kindred spirits. Soon they were fast friends and the fallen Isis was given the position of nurse to the Queen's infant son. The love that Isis felt for the child was immediate so she resolved to make the boy immortal. Each night the beggar-goddess gave the child her finger to suck to take away all distress. Then she built a great fire in the hall and into its fierce blaze she placed the boy while transforming herself into a swallow the better to fan the flames. Such goings-on could not be kept a secret in the intrigues of the court so the Queen, having heard disturbing rumours, hid herself within the hall and, witnessing the nurse place her child in the fire, gave a shriek and leapt forward to snatch her beloved son from the flames.

At this, Isis grew angry and revealed herself in her true form as a goddess of the line of Ra. Divine light shone from every pore of her body. 'Oh weak and foolish mortal woman, know you not that I am Isis of the many names, mistress of magic? And that by your rash action you have deprived your son of the gift of immortality.'

Still shaking with terror, the Queen begged the goddess's forgiveness. 'How is it that I may atone for my sin?' she cried.

By now the wrath of Isis had ebbed and had turned to weeping. 'Give to me the central pillar of your hall,' she said simply. Nodding, the shocked Queen gave her assent. Isis now stretched forth her hands and the wood of the pillar flew apart to reveal the gorgeously appointed coffer which Set had made.

CROWNS

CROWNS AND head-dresses had a potent significance in Ancient Egyptian royal symbolism. The Two Lands of Upper and Lower Egypt, over which the Pharaoh had dominion, were each identified by a distinctive crown. The diadem of Lower Egypt was flat and red in colour and is often called the Mortar of the North. The crown of the Upper Land, being tall and white, is described as the Mitre of the South. These crowns were either worn as individual items of apparel or together, the white crown fitting neatly within the red.

In addition to these dominant symbols, the Pharaoh also wore different crowns for specific occasions, which probably represented his affinity with individual gods. The Blue Crown or Khepresh, for instance, was only worn by the ruler in times of war, or for military events.

The Great Royal Wife had her own particular head-dresses. The Vulture Crown, for example, was an emblem of the goddesses Nekhebet, Isis and Mut who were regarded as motherly influences shading their young from the heat of the sun.

A ship was made available to the goddess so she, with the body of her husband, returned to Egypt. The remnants of the great pillar were reverently placed in a temple dedicated to Isis at Byblos, and there they remained as sacred relics for evermore.

Landing at the delta, Isis concealed the chest in a thicket while she repaired to the place where she kept her most closely guarded secret. Retrieving a small box, the goddess opened it to take out some clay which she had preserved for many years. For Isis had once cared for the mighty Ra himself when he was old and infirm and this very clay had been spat upon by the god. With great care Isis moulded the damp earth into the semblance of an asp with a head like an arrow and, just as Ra had done in the beginning of things, she named it and by her word the serpent lived.

Now Isis knew that Ra, even though he no longer dwelt on earth, occasionally visited to walk on the land which he had created. So Isis, soothing the serpent all the while, came to a crossroad upon which Ra would tread. Depositing her venomous creation there, she hid herself and prepared to wait. At length the light of the sun was dimmed in comparison to the golden glow that emanated from the godly figure of Ra himself who came surrounded by a retinue of lesser deities. On reaching the crossroad, the great god paused. At that moment the serpent, mindful of its mistress's instructions, struck – sinking its dripping fangs into the ankle of Ra. The scream of Ra echoed throughout creation. 'What has struck me?' cried the god in agony. At this, those in his entourage gathered round, bewildered, but Ra was now silent for he had sunk to the earth as a terrible weakness overcame him.

The jaws of the mighty creator now chattered and his whole body shook as the spasms of agony lanced through his godly form. There he lay quivering in the dust, the lord of all creation. Eventually, Ra gained enough self-possession to speak through clenched teeth. 'Come all of you, come all gods who were made from my will and I will tell you what has happened to me.'

At Ra's words the gods gathered around their ancestor, Thoth taking the lead and bending to catch the sun-god's words. 'I have been fearfully wounded,' croaked Ra, 'I know in my heart that this is so, yet my eyes did not see the thing that has caused me such grievous pain, and I swear by my secret name that I did not create it.'

'Then what could possibly harm you so?' asked Thoth.

'I know not,' gasped the sun-god, 'yet if its name cannot be found out then I will eternally suffer. For I burn like a fire and am as cold as the depths of a well. My limbs shake like the boughs of a tree in a storm and my mouth is as dry as the desert sand.' Then Thoth commanded the presence of all the gods with knowledge of magic.

Again did Ra speak. 'Call for Isis, my great-granddaughter for she alone has the skill to save me from eternal pain.'

Amidst the mourning and lamentations of the gods came Isis who spoke to Ra saying, 'What is this O first ancestor? Has any serpent or other creation of your hand dared to raise its head against you?'

'No being of mine has struck me so,' moaned Ra. 'I passed over the Two Lands and a serpent that I saw not struck me with its fangs. Was it fire? Was it water? For I am hotter than fire and colder than water, my limbs quake and sweat bathes my face as it does the faces of men in the heat of summer.'

'Then this venom shall be overcome by the might of my magic,' replied Isis, 'and I will drive it out by means of your own glory. Now, first father, tell me your true name that I may cast a potent spell to end your pain.'

Ra then glared at Isis growling, 'I am the maker of heaven and earth, and all that is beneath the earth. I am the establisher of the mountains. I am the creator of the waters. I am the maker of the secrets of the two horizons. I am light and I am darkness. I create the hours, I create the days. I am the opener of festivals. I make the running streams and the living flames. I am Khepera in the morning, I am Ra at noontide and I am Atum at dusk. In the darkness of night I am Efu-Ra in the under-earth, my face is that of Aten the sun's disc; and many are my names in other lands.'

CHRONICLES OF ANCIENT EGYPT

Coolly Isis began her chant calling on the venom to leave the body of Ra. First she called it to submit to the power of the name of Khepera, but Ra still groaned and shook. She then called on the power of the name of Atum but still the great god quaked. Then in turn, she spoke the many names of the sun-god but to none of them would the poison yield.

'Lord Creator,' intoned the goddess, 'this evil will not depart by the power of these names. Surely there is another mightier yet, which will triumph.'

'There is one,' agreed the suffering god, 'but that name is engraved upon my very heart and possesses the powers of creation. Never has it been spoken since the very universe was new. It is my secret name from which all my godly strength flows.'

'Then if you will not reveal it to me, there is nought that I can do to alleviate your suffering,' said Isis.

Ra was silent save for moans of torment. At length Isis spoke again, 'Tell me your secret name, which is your true name, not these others which all men know. Only then will I be able to heal you by the might of my magic.'

By now the fire of the poison had consumed the sun-god's will. With an almighty effort he rose unsteadily to his feet calling for Isis to support him. 'Let Isis come with me and away from these other gods for what is to pass between us is for we two alone.' At this, Isis half carried the weakened Ra some distance from the rest of the assembly. Then did Ra conceal himself and Isis from the watching eyes so that it seemed they no longer existed. Only when he was sure that they were not spied upon or overheard did Ra open his heart and allow his secret name to pass into Isis. Thus did Isis gain the title She of the Many Names for she now shared with Ra the primordial power of creation.

Then, in this hidden place, Isis spoke to Ra as an equal. 'Bind yourself with an oath O Ra,' she demanded, 'that you will give the power of your eyes to my son Horus who is not yet born.'

'That I will,' replied the creator. 'I swear it. In return you O Isis will share my name with only one other. That one is to be Horus who is not yet born.' To this condition Isis readily agreed. Then, calling upon her magic, she spoke aloud the secret name of Ra in which all the powers of creation are enfolded. At once the burning coldness of the asp's venom departed from Ra and he was whole once more.

Bowing low before Ra in the full company of the gods Isis took her leave for now she had the power of life and death. Mightier than ever were her enchantments for she was now the skilful healer, and her very words conquered pain. In her mouth was the very breath of creation and by it she could raise the dead. Knowing this, the goddess hastened back to the delta to restore her husband Osiris to life once more.

Triumphantly did Isis return to the place where she had hidden the coffer containing her husband's body, but on coming to the thicket she was horrified to find that the casket had been breached and Osiris's body was nowhere to be found.

Again did Isis sit dejected in the Nile mud and weep, for all the power that she had gained now seemed for nought.

In her lamentations Isis did not hear the approach of her sister Nephthys and the infant Anubis. 'Oh sister,' said Nephthys, 'yet again it is the malice of Set that is to blame for this outrage. He was hunting in the delta when he came upon the coffer. He opened it and in his rage became a wild animal and tore the corpse of your husband to pieces, scattering them far and wide so now nought can be done to bring our beloved Osiris to eternal rest.'

Then the eyes of Isis became cold and she ceased her mourning. 'Osiris does not rest and neither shall we, for we will seek out the poor sundered remnants of his body and restore him. I now possess the breath of creation and I tell you that Osiris will live again.' Thus did Isis begin her second wanderings, accompanied by dark Nephthys and jackal-headed Anubis.

In a reed boat, the three made their way through the delta towards the source of the sacred Nile. All the beasts of the earth and the birds of the air heard the call of Isis as far away as Nubia and searched with her. And truly is it said that ever after, those who sailed in a boat of reeds were safe from the ravages of crocodiles for the scaly creatures think that the weary goddess is still questing for the body of Osiris.

For many years did they search evading the vengeance of Set who still ruled as god and King. Each time a fragment of the sundered god Osiris was found, Isis would build a lovely shrine and perform the funeral rites as though she had just buried her

husband. At Abydos his head is said to lie, while on an island at the Elephantine, his right leg is rumoured to be entombed. Of this last, some believe that it is from the decaying seepage of this limb that the headwaters of the Nile flow instead of from the caverns of Khnum. In truth, Isis took each part with her giving them over to Anubis, who with an embalmer's skill joined the fragments again, anointing each with oils and spices and wrapping them all in bandages. In this way did Anubis, jackal-headed lord of graves invent the arts of mummification.

Only one part of Osiris eluded Isis in her long search. This was the god's phallus, which had been swallowed by an oxyrhynchus fish. Finally admitting to her defeat, Isis created by magic a substitute phallus. This, too, was joined to the embalmed body of the god by Anubis as Isis breathed the breath of creation into the corpse's nostrils. Then, by the power of the name of Ra which Isis had stolen, did Osiris awake from death.

But since Osiris was not truly whole he could not be restored to earthly existence but must reign as god and king over the dead in the lands of the farthest west where the sun sets. However, before he passed through the Gates of Night, Osiris lay with Isis and by the power of his fertility ensured that she was with child. Henceforth, Isis would give her love and loyalty to her son Horus and instil in him his destiny: utterly to defeat the vile Set and to sit upon the throne of his father, to rule with justice and wisdom.

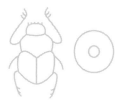

The two goddesses, Isis the pure and faithful widow and dark Nephthys the discarded wife of Set, were triumphant for Osiris lived eternally and was a king once more. Yet they were sad at the departure of the benevolent god from their world. They had given no thought to their own fates but cared only for the departed Osiris and the unborn son of Isis who, by the will of Ra, was to be named Horus.

So it was that Set, who still reigned as the Lord of the Two Lands, came upon the pair as they walked on the banks of the Nile. Set stood tall and proud in his chariot surrounded by a retinue of flatterers.

'Is it fitting that a pharaoh of Egypt should allow two of his kinswomen to wander like beggars in the wilderness?' asked the cunning god.

'No my lord, it is not fitting, but it is you who have brought us to this state of penury,' answered Isis, who stood proudly despite the discomfort of her pregnancy.

'Then you shall be beggars no longer,' laughed Set, 'for I will provide you the

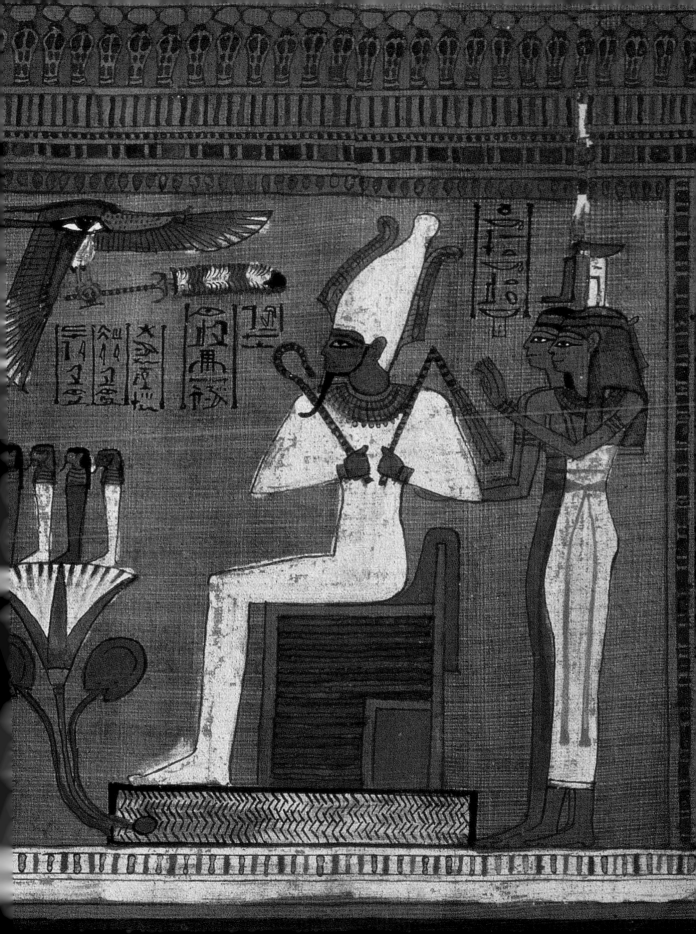

means to earn your own bread and to make your way in the world as respectable widows.' So saying, Set struck his asses cruelly with a whip and sped off, leaving Isis and Nephthys choking in his dust. They were taken to a house of women and there set to spin flax for their daily ration of bread. Long months passed as the belly of Isis grew round and her time of deliverance grew near.

Sometimes, Set would taunt the pair. 'Is it true that now my brother Osiris reigns as king in the Land of the Dead?' he enquired.

'That is so,' replied Isis, refusing to look up.

'The dead are fitting company for one who had so little conversation,' quipped Set. 'I prefer to rule the living as I shall do for evermore.'

On another occasion Set came to spread his malice again. 'Brother Osiris should be grateful to me.'

'Why would my lord, the noble Osiris, have cause for gratitude?' asked Isis.

'Why I add to his kingdom daily,' laughed the evil Set.

At length a boy was born to Isis in captivity. The child she named Horus, who is called Horus the Younger to distinguish him from his noble uncle who acts as steersman in the Boat of Ra. Now Set did not at first wish to kill the boy but desired to corrupt him as he had already done with Babai who was another son of Osiris by a concubine. So Isis continued to spin and care for her baby while Set would come to taunt her until even that petty pleasure ceased to amuse him.

One day, Isis sat at her spinning while Horus lay in a basket at her feet. She did not look up when a shadow fell across the door for she thought that Set had again come to make sport of her. Then a gentle hand lifted her face and she looked into the divine visage of Thoth the Wise, scribe of the gods, the measurer of time.

'By the will of Ra have you suffered for the trick you played on him,' began the god. 'Now it is time you left this place and fled the power of Set. Take the child with you for when he is grown and his strength developed you will place him on the throne of his father, and the rulership of the Two Lands will be given over to him.' So spoke the voice of Thoth, most sagacious of the gods, as he vanished from her presence.

Needing no further encouragement, Isis picked up her baby and walked from the house of spinning. As she walked she expected at any moment to be apprehended by the guards of Set but nothing happened. No sentinel questioned her, nor did anyone attempt to impede her flight for Thoth had prevented any from seeing Isis depart. However, Isis knew that this spell would soon break so she used her own magic to summon seven scorpions as guardians to follow and to slay any who pursued her and her son. And these were named Mestet, Mestetef, Petet, Thetet, Matet, Befen and Tefenet. The mightiest of these was Tefenet who bore the poisons of all the others upon her venomous sting.

Once they were gathered, Isis spoke. 'Beware of Set the Black One, call not Set the Red One, look neither at children nor at any small helpless creature. Take care not to leave any clue to my path until we reach the marshes of the delta.'

Once before, Isis had sought sanctuary in the lands of the delta. It was to that marshy place she again set her feet, travelling mostly by night with Tefenet and Befen covering her retreat, Mestet and Mestetef at her side and Petet, Thetet and Matet going before. She hid during the day, soothing her child with her finger to keep him quiet and content, and hence the infant Horus is regarded as the god of silence.

It was with relief that Isis came to the city of Crocodilopolis, and then to the Town of the Two Sandals for it is at these places that the swamps and marshes of the northland begins. The goddess, child and scorpion entourage entered the fields of papyrus and made for the primitive settlements of the swamp people.

A chieftain's wife named Usert was the first to see the noble lady bearing a child and surrounded by scorpions. With insulting words, she called Isis a foul witch and would not let her rest in the settlement even though her weariness was plain for all to see. So onward went the small procession until Isis and her son found refuge in the humble hut of a fisherwoman. There the goddess lay down to sleep on a mat of woven reeds. And while she slept the guardian scorpions spoke together for the insulting words of Usert the chieftain's wife had hurt their pride. Tefenet, the most venomous of the seven, resolved to avenge herself. Moving swiftly upon her eight stout legs, Tefenet went to the house of the chieftain, slipped beneath the door and stung the woman's son. So potent was her poison, having the seven-fold strength of her companions, that the very vapour of it ignited into flame setting the house on fire. Satisfied, the scorpion Tefenet returned to the side of Isis.

Now Usert had been woken by the spitting of the flames. She snatched up her son and fled into the night but only when she had set the boy down did she see that he was blue with the scorpion's venom. Loudly she lamented but no man or woman came to her aid. However, across the watercourses Isis heard her cries, as she does for all, and came swiftly. She did not care about the insults the woman had shouted.

'My father has taught me the secret of driving out poison,' she said softly.

Isis then placed her hands on the child's fever-wracked body and called on her magical powers to save him. 'O poison of Tefenet come out,' she cried. 'Come out of him and fall upon the ground. Poison of Befen advance not, penetrate no farther, come out of him and fall upon the ground. Venom of Mestet hasten not. Venom of Mestetef rise not. Venom of Petet and Thetet approach not. Venom of Matet come out and fall upon the ground for did I not instruct you to look not on children or any other harmless thing? For I am Isis, mistress of magic, speaker of spells whose voice can awake the dead. The child shall live, the poison shall die. As Horus is strong and well for me, so shall this child be strong and well for his mother.'

At the words of Isis the child stirred and was well again, the fire was extinguished and the thankful Usert fell at the goddess's feet.

Now it was time for Isis and her son Horus to move on lest Set and his minions of evil find them. In time they came to Khemmis near to the Great Green Sea. This was a poor place of stagnant watercourses dotted with small islands, uncultivated and sparsely populated. But it was here that Isis felt safe. Life at Khemmis was hard, yet Isis was rewarded by the baby Horus growing into a lively youngster. So it was with regret that Isis had daily to leave her child so she could forage and beg for food.

One day Isis returned to their humble abode to discover Horus lying cold and lifeless on the ground. All the horror of the death of her husband returned to her and

ATEN

THE MOST eccentric member of the Eighteenth Dynasty was Amenophis IV who is better known to posterity by his self-chosen name of Akhenaten (*d.* 1336 BC). This king abandoned the ancient religion of his forebears and adopted a new god Aten, the sun's disc, as his sole deity.

Unlike all other gods in the Ancient Egyptian belief system, this new divinity was never personified as a person or an animal but was always shown as a golden disc from which descended benevolent rays, each ending in a human hand in the gesture of blessing.

The cult of Aten superseded all other worship including that of the previously supreme deity Amun-Ra. Akhenaten's

fanaticism in his newly created religion was such that he eventually proscribed the worship of any other god but his own, and mismanaged the realm so completely that whole provinces fell to the enemies of Egypt.

There was a reversion to the old gods of Egypt under Akhenaten's son Tutankhaten, whose name was changed, with the revival of the old religion, to the more familiar Tutankhamun (*d.* 1325 BC).

Akhenaten has gone down in history as the 'heretic' pharaoh despite the efforts of the powerful priests of Amun to obliterate his name completely. So thorough were they in this endeavour that Akhenaten was known as 'The Great Criminal' and no trace of his mummy has ever been found.

Isis felt that she was descending into madness once more. In this terrible state all her magical knowledge was lost to her and she was unable to heal her son. Calling for help, Isis nursed the limp bundle and realized that the guileful Set had sent a snake or some other venomous thing to slay her child.

'Horus has been bitten, Horus has been bitten,' she lamented. 'The beautiful, sinless, fatherless child has been bitten. He is the son of the god whom I tended, he was to be the avenger of his father. Horus has been bitten, Horus has been bitten.'

So anguished were her cries that they summoned both her sister Nephthys, who had also escaped Set, and the scorpion-goddess Selkis. These two were as horrified as Isis and, at first, could think of nothing that would help. Then Selkis was the first to speak.

'Here we are, three powerful goddesses. Let us together call upon the Boat of Ra to halt in the heavens until things are well with Horus once more.'

So the three used their divine will to halt the boat of the sun. At once time stopped. The light of the sun was dimmed. A droplet falling from a leaf paused in its descent. The sacred Nile ceased to flow and the birds of the air hovered upon stilled wings.

Far above in the Boat of Millions of Years ibis-headed Thoth, the measurer of time, was perturbed. Descending by magic he called out, 'O Isis what have you done?'

The sobbing Isis could not speak so Selkis replied. 'Great Thoth, twice magnified in the favour of Ra, the child Horus lies still and dead, a serpent's fangs have snatched his life.'

'And this has been done by the will of the vile Set,' added Nephthys.

'Do not fear ladies,' said Thoth, 'for I have a spell which will cure the blessed child.' Then Thoth the Wise began to intone: 'Horus may your heart be strong. Your protection is he who is in the sun disc, who rules heaven, who gives light to the Two Lands. He is your guardian in his many forms. Awake Horus, for your protection is everlasting. Out poison. The mighty god Ra drives you away. His boat stands still and will not move until the patient is recovered. The wells are dry, the crops wither and food is snatched from men, until Horus is restored to health for his mother Isis. Your spirit is your protection and your attendants guard you. The poison is dead, its force is dispelled. Horus lives to his mother's delight.'

49

Thus spoke Thoth, his arms spread wide, and at his words the child Horus stirred and returned to life coughing up the poison which had so afflicted him. And these words may be spoken over any who are similarly wounded by the bite of a serpent.

Weeping with gratitude Isis prostrated herself before the god of wisdom. Thoth then bade the three goddesses farewell with these words, 'Watch over this child and divert his enemies until the day comes when he can assume the throne of his father.'

He then ascended once more to resume his station at the side of Ra. Thereafter whenever Isis was absent, the young Horus was tended by the cobra-goddess Wadjet who in the time of mortals was to be seen on the brow of pharaohs to remind the world that they too were Horus. As a reward for this action Ra made Wadjet the goddess of the North and bestowed the Red Crown of that land upon her.

As a further precaution, the goddesses Isis, Nephthys and Selkis ensured that the island upon which Horus was hidden was cast adrift in the sea so that the evil Set might never find it. These things done Isis was content to wait until Horus was grown enough to be taken before the court of the gods.

When the boy Horus was grown sturdy and strong the goddess Isis, his doting mother, considered him old enough to be brought before the court of the Nine Gods of Heliopolis, the chief of whom was the mighty Ra himself. There he would stand as the accuser of his red-headed uncle Set, the murderer of his father Osiris, and usurper of his throne.

Word was brought to Isis that the entire company of gods was to meet on an island in the delta not far from where she and her son had concealed themselves for many years. So, the two journeyed there and were conveyed to the meeting place by the ferryman Anty.

The gods, Shu, Tefnut, Geb, Nut, Thoth, Horus the Elder, Nephthys and Set sat enthroned about the regal place reserved for the awesome presence of Ra. Further back stood a multitude of lesser gods and spirits all in attendance to the great ones. It was before this august assemblage that Isis and the young Horus came.

In ringing tones Isis addressed the company: 'I am Isis daughter of Geb and Nut, once Queen of the Two Lands. I am a goddess of the line of Ra and am known by many names. I come before you to appeal for justice for my son who has been dispossessed of all that he should own by a foul liar and murderer who even now sits amongst you.'

At this Set rose to his feet. 'If my sitting displeases my sister Isis so much then I will stand even as she does before this company. Let her make her accusations then and let her be judged for her rash presumption.'

'On this occasion I am not the accuser of Set,' said Isis coldly. 'That duty belongs to the son of the god that was so wronged, namely my son Horus who is the true Pharaoh of the Two Lands.'

'What is this nonsense?' demanded Set, as a murmur passed around the assembly of gods. 'This is but a callow boy without the strength in him to command nations.'

'Boy I may be,' replied Horus, 'but I, too, am of the line of Ra uncle, and I accuse you of murder and usurpation. Furthermore you are guilty of desecration of the dead and of imprisoning my mother and attempting to murder me while I still lay helpless in my crib.'

Before Set could respond with a foul jibe, the god Shu, son of Ra, rose to his feet. 'Before us stands my grandson Set, and my great-grandson Horus who is the son of Osiris. All here would freely admit that the boy's father Osiris was the true Pharaoh, thus his son also should inherit all that was his father's. Yet Set has been a strong king and it is no idle thing to depose such a one. Even so, my sympathies are with Horus, for if we do not decide in his favour then where are the just ways of Maat?'

'Maat has gone with Osiris into the underworld,' spat Set. 'The might of my arm rules now, and justice is nothing.'

Now Thoth who had ever favoured the cause of Horus spoke. 'Set speaks truth, as he understands it, yet in memory of Maat we should follow her ways. Thus I say that the cause of Horus is a just one and has been amply proved to my satisfaction.' All the gods then turned to Ra in expectation. The shining one cleared his throat and looked distinctly uncomfortable as he rose to give judgement.

'It is a heavy thing,' began Ra, 'to judge between two of my descendants, but it is a duty that I will not shirk.' The gods sighed with satisfaction. 'Whereas right and lawful vengeance are on the side of the youthful Horus, he is still a boy and it is not fitting that one so young should take up the burdens of state. I have decided that Set shall continue to reign but that Horus should be declared his heir.' The gods began to mutter for this was not the solution that they had in mind.

Isis glowered at her ancestor Ra, Horus was speechless with anger, but it was Set who roared: 'This is not acceptable for I have sworn to rule the world for all time. I accept the verdict of Ra, yet I will now challenge Horus to a contest of strength to prove once and for all the boy is not worthy.'

'I accept your challenge, uncle, now and forever,' shouted Horus.

Then Thoth held up his hands. 'My lords,' he cried, 'this is a matter of principle. Surely it can be resolved here with the gods in conference.'

'These words are not acceptable,' objected Set. 'Let the matter be decided by a contest between Horus and myself.'

'I will fight you at any time,' answered Horus.

'Battle was not my intent,' Set smoothly continued. 'Rather, let us both take on the form of hippopotami and immerse ourselves in the waters. There we will remain without the blessing of air, until one of us rises to the surface for breath. That one, and I have no doubt that it will be the feeble Horus, will be adjudged the loser, and the other will be acclaimed King of the Two Lands.'

The assembly of gods gave a sigh of relief for, this way, war might be avoided. Calling on their powers the two gods, Set and Horus, waded into the shallows. Once they were far enough from shore both adopted the form of a lumbering hippopotamus. With a wary eye one on the other, both sank from sight.

The gods continued to watch the empty waves for some time before drifting away to their own concerns. Only Isis remained for she suspected further treachery from her false brother and was determined to meet it with treachery of her own. She waited for five days and began to fear that her son had met with some misfortune. With this in mind the goddess stood ready on the bank armed with a harpoon, holding tightly to its rope. She was ready to deal a death blow to Set as he rose from the water. Before too long her patience was rewarded by the sight of bubbles on the surface. Convinced that these came from Set she drew back her arm and threw with all her might. The harpoon struck home and the hippopotamus that was Horus reared in agony from the waves. Swiftly the goddess realized her error and pulling the rope she freed her son from his agony. Now further disturbance indicated the presence of Set. Again Isis threw the harpoon. Her aim was true and the red hippopotamus, who was Set, was impaled by the wicked dart.

Groaning in agony, the beast crawled on to the shore at the feet of Isis. Returning to his

normal form Set lay there gasping as Isis raised the harpoon one further time intent on ending the villain's life.

'Strike not dear sister,' gasped Set, 'for were we not born of the same womb?'

Then did Isis hesitate and the weapon fall from her grasp. Swiftly, Set was on his feet and, calling on his godly strength, fled the scene. At this Horus threw off his animal form and attacked his mother.

'Foolish woman, our enemy was in your hands and you have allowed him to escape,' he shouted. So great was the anger of Horus that he drew his sword and sliced off her head. But this was not the end of Isis for, seeing the blade approach, she transformed herself into a statue made of flint so that the head that was severed was made of nothing more than stone. It was with this that Horus, still mad with rage, fled to the mountains.

Some time later the mighty Ra and the wise Thoth were taking their ease on the shore of the Nile.

'Who has made this form with no head?' asked Ra, on seeing the headless statue.

'I fear that it must be Isis who has fallen foul of the combatants,' replied Thoth.

But Ra knew that it was none other than her own son who had done this terrible deed. 'Call to the gods,' he commanded. 'Let this unnatural boy Horus be found and brought to justice.'

At these words, the wounded Set came forth. 'I swear that I will be the one to find him.'

Ra smiled on Set. 'And in return I will confirm you in your right to the throne.' At this the company of gods set out to find Horus, with the limping Set close behind.

It was indeed Set who found the boy as he lay sleeping in a mountainous ravine. Giving Horus no chance to arm himself the red god leapt upon his enemy and with his fingers gouged out the boy's eyes. Ignoring the agonized screams of Horus, Set took up the stone head of Isis and together with the bleeding orbs of the eyes, returned with them to the court of Ra. There, by the wisdom of Thoth counter of the stars, the head and body of Isis were restored and she lived again.

Now the gentle goddess Hathor, daughter of the sun, had become enamoured of the golden

Horus so she too sought him in the wilderness. However, it was not the glorious hero of her imagination that she found but a bleeding boy, maimed and blind. Then Hathor comforted Horus and promised him her love. Using magic she caught a female gazelle and milked it. Then she applied the milk to her lover's eye sockets and soon new eyes had formed in the inky blackness and Horus could see once more. Lovely Hathor then took Horus by the hand and led him to the court so all the gods were again assembled.

Then spoke Ra. 'The last contest between Horus and Set was fairly won by the red god, for reason of the treachery of Isis, who was repaid for her deed by an act of violence committed by her own son. Such a one as Horus is not worthy of the throne therefore Set remains as King.'

'I will not submit to your verdict,' raged Horus.

Then Ra grew angry with Horus roaring, 'You foolish boy, you are too rash and feeble to hold the throne of your father. You cannot sustain royal estate. Go away for you have still your mother's milk in your mouth.'

The company of gods were horrified by this attack on Horus but held their tongues for fear of Ra. Then one, a minor god named Babai who was a son of Osiris, but who had been raised by Set shouted, 'Who are you Ra? Who on earth listens to your senile drivel any more? Your shrines are neglected by men who have moved on to more powerful gods.'

At this outburst Ra rose to his feet so full of anger that he was unable to speak. The stunned god then stormed from the assembly and returned to his pavilion where he sat brooding alone, refusing companionship.

The assembly of gods turned on Babai speaking as with a single voice, 'You have committed a terrible crime against our ancestor Ra. Go now to your father in the underworld.' Thus did Babai pass through the Gates of Night to the judgement chamber of Maat where he still remains, subsisting on the entrails of the damned.

Now the company of the gods was alarmed, for without Ra no judgement could be given and the simmering conflict between Set and Horus would erupt once more. Then Hathor, Ra's lovely cow-eyed daughter, the goddess of desire, entered the tent of her father and displayed herself naked before him. Thus did Hathor turn one passion, that of rage, to another and revived the lost pride of Ra. The sun-god came forth ordering that the two claimants present their cases before him once more.

Set slammed down his fist declaring, 'I am Set the Red, mightiest of the company of gods. I have slain the enemies of Ra and no other god can do this. I deserve the throne of Osiris and mean to hold on to it.'

So passionate was his speech that many of the assembled gods were swayed and cried, 'Set is in the right, let him keep the throne.'

Now Thoth and Onuris, the far-travelled god of hunting, shouted together, 'It is wrong that this high position should be given to a brother on the mother's side while a son of Osiris's body is still alive.'

The company of the gods began to mutter amongst themselves, some favouring the cause of Horus, and others that of Set. Now Ra's wrath burned fiercely again. 'Never before have my decisions been questioned,' he thundered. 'This matter threatens to overturn the order of the universe.'

The far-travelled Onuris stepped forward then and spoke. 'Let us ask the wise Banebdedet, the ram-god of the city of Mendes, his opinion otherwise conflict will come again. I for one am ready to fight, for the cause of Horus is just, yet sober counsel must prevail.'

At this suggestion Ra smiled. 'Let it be so, for then the verdict is out of my hands.'

The ram Banebdedet, however, was equally loath to decide between the two claimants and advised the court to write to the ancient goddess Neith the huntress. This goddess was a close blood relative of Ra himself, second only to him in age and a mighty being whose judgement would be fair and just.

The task of writing the letter fell to Thoth who, as scribe to the gods, set down the words of Ra: 'My mind is much troubled. I lie awake with no hope of sleep considering the problem of the successor of Osiris. Every day I take counsel with the Two Lands trying to resolve the problem. What are we to do with these two contenders who have brought their claims to the nine gods? None knows how to judge between them. Answer dear sister I pray.'

The letter was dispatched to the sanctuary of Neith the Ancient at Sais. Some claim her to be the mother of Ra, or at the very least his sister. On reading it she laid down her bow and darts, shaking her head in despair. Taking brush and papyrus she carefully worded her reply: 'In answer O Ra, I say that it is clear that the throne of the Two Lands be given to Horus by right of his birth. And to Horus and Set I say, "Refrain from making war one upon the other and cease those wicked deeds which are inappropriate for descendants of Ra. If you do not I will rage and I will bring the sky crashing down upon you both."'

It was with some amusement that Ra read his sister's words, but saw the benefit to be gained from her wisdom. So, when next the gods met, Ra solemnly confirmed the throne upon the triumphant Horus. To prevent the revenge of the dispossessed Set, he offered the red-headed god a doubling of his earthly possessions and marriage to two of Ra's adopted daughters, the Syrian goddesses Astarte and Anath. These two presented themselves to Set. The beautiful Astarte, the Lady of Horses, arrived in her splendid war-chariot, naked yet armed for battle. Then came Anath, as lovely as her sister, wearing the White Crown and bearing a mace and shield. About her shoulders was draped the skin of an exotic panther. As the lustful eyes of Set fell upon these two paragons, his resolve faltered and he accepted the terms of Ra and unwillingly resigned the throne to his nephew. Now Ra made the pronouncement that the young Horus was to be installed as Pharaoh of the Two Lands. At these words Set's resolve returned and his face turned black with rage.

Horus then humbly addressed the shining Ra. 'O ancestor, it is said that by gazing into your eye the future may be revealed. Have I your permission to approach?'

'Look deep my boy, and see what is to be revealed,' replied the King of the gods.

Now, though Set had relinquished his throne, he did not have any intention of allowing Horus to enjoy his victory. Muttering dark spells, the vile Set took upon himself the form of a black pig of fierce aspect with the fury of the thunderstorm in his eyes. This pig then slowly walked by Ra and Horus. At its passing Ra exclaimed, 'Look at that monstrous boar. Never have I seen one so huge and terrible.'

At these words Horus turned and, as he did so, the pig-Set sent a bolt of fire from his bloody eyes into those of Horus. At once a burning agony overcame the youthful god and he fell to his knees screaming, 'It is Set who has smitten me and destroyed my sight once more.'

Then Ra laid a curse on the pig as it fled into a thicket. 'Let this beast be an abomination for all time.' So ever afterward the flesh of the pig was forbidden to men and boars were sacrificed every full moon.

Then Thoth, the most wise divider of the hours, came swiftly to the pair and healed the eyes of Horus by spitting upon them. Without further delay, Horus armed himself and went in pursuit of Set. He came upon him in the desert and fierce battle commenced, but victory was denied to each. Again Set struck at the face of Horus, damaging his left eye while, for his part, it is said that Horus grievously wounded Set's testicles rendering him barren.

When next the two rivals came to the court of Ra, the ancient god ruled that since peace was impossible no matter what decision he made, then the Two Lands should indeed be divided. To Horus he allotted Lower Egypt and the fertile lands of the delta. To Set went the wild country of desert and scrub of Upper Egypt.

Horus then cried out, 'I have been tricked for it is less than one day since the Two Crowns were bestowed upon me.'

Isis too raged. 'I will not rest until both the Crowns sit upon my son's head.'

'My sister's words and spells are mighty so that the gods are persuaded by her,' growled Set, 'yet if any think that I will surrender to her will, then these I will slay with my weighty staff. If Isis remains here then I will not for my days of speech-making are done.' So saying, the furious Set departed the assembly.

Sighing, the great god Ra, spoke. 'Go after him you gods and bring him to a near-by island. There too this assembly shall meet, but it is my will that Isis be barred from the proceedings. Instruct the ferryman Anty that he is not to convey her or any woman across the water.'

So it was that the entire company of gods was ferried to a new site leaving Isis smouldering with frustrated rage as she watched them go.

Taking the form of an old peasant woman, Isis came to Anty the ferryman. 'Will you take me across to the island young man?' she enquired. 'I bring a pot of flour

for a boy who has been tending cattle there and who must be hungry by now.'

'The mighty Ra himself has instructed me to ferry no woman to the island for fear of the magic of Isis,' replied Anty.

'But I am no goddess or enchantress either,' said the hag. 'What harm is there?'

'What will you give me as toll?' asked Anty.

'You may have this loaf of bread,' replied the disguised Isis.

'Do you call that a toll?' the ferryman scoffed.

'Very well, I will give you this small gold ring which is the only thing of value I own for I am a poor widow,' said the cunning Isis.

Greedily Anty took the ring and, with no further questions, helped the old woman into the boat and rowed to the island.

Bidding Anty farewell, Isis crept through the papyrus reeds until she could see the gods at their meal. The great ones were talking amongst themselves so did not notice the movement of the reeds. Set alone was watchful so Isis transformed herself into a beautiful mortal girl the better to catch his ever-lustful eye. Slowly, Isis showed herself and then fled from his sight. His passions roused, Set gave chase. Long did Set pursue the girl until Isis, pretending mortal weakness, rested gasping by a tree. Set slyly came up behind her whispering, 'I am close beside you, fair lady.'

59

'Oh my lord do me no wrong,' whimpered Isis, 'for I am in distress.'

'And why would such a pretty young girl be distressed?' said Set drawing closer.

'Oh sir, I was the wife of a cow-herd who died when young. To him I bore a son, who has now grown, but when he went to claim his father's cattle as was his right, a stranger came and took the entire herd.'

'That is terrible,' said Set.

'It is not the worst of it,' moaned the girl, 'for this stranger has sworn to beat my son and turn him from his father's house.'

'This is a thing that I will not allow, for I am King of the Two Lands and I swear that I will act on your behalf for it is not right that property be given up to a stranger when a true heir is still alive.'

'Now you have condemned yourself out of your own mouth,' shouted Isis transforming herself into a kite. Realizing he had been tricked, Set ran to Ra complaining that Isis had taken unfair advantage of his hot-blooded nature. Ra had little sympathy, so the red-headed god seized Anty the ferryman and painfully flayed the soles of his feet. This is the reason that Anty, ferryman to the gods, swore that he would never again take his fare in gold.

To Horus Set sent a message, saying: 'There has been enough contention between us. Come nephew, let us put our rivalry aside and join me at my pavilion for a feast.' When Horus read the letter he resolved to go if only to show Set that the bright god was not afraid. Isis, however, advised her son not to go, but Horus would not be swayed.

So it was that Horus and Set sat together eating and drinking and when dense darkness fell, lay down together in the same bed. Now vile Set had evil in his mind so while Horus slept he mounted his nephew to thrust his seed into the body of Horus. But Horus placed his hand between his thighs and caught the seed of Set in his palm. Set arose satisfied, for he thought he had now made Horus a woman.

The next morning, Horus went to his mother showing her what Set had done. Taking a sharp knife, Isis severed the offending hand and conjured another from the bleeding stump to take its place. The severed hand, Set's seed and all, were thrown into the marsh. Then Isis used her hand to bring forth the seed of Horus which she concealed beneath her robe. The goddess then made her way to the garden of Set to engage the gardener in conversation. 'Tell me good fellow,' began Isis, 'which vegetables does my brother Set eat?'

'The Lord Set eats only the lettuce,' replied the gardener. When his back was turned Isis allowed the drops of Horus's seed to fall on the plant. Happy now, Isis returned to the court to wait for Set's next action.

It was not long before a blustering Set came before the gods demanding that the trial be begun again. 'Now have I won the contest for it is evident that Horus is my inferior for he has my seed within his body.' The gods gasped at this accusation and agreed that if this was true then Set must be adjudged the winner. The clever Thoth, though, was privy to the secret and asked Set to call forth his seed from Horus.

Laughing, Set extended his power, calling, 'Where are you, my seed?'

'I am here O my creator,' answered a voice from the marsh.

Again Set had been tricked and he made to leave but Isis held him. 'Now let Horus call forth his seed to answer,' she demanded. Horus called on his seed which spoke from the belly of Set, for he had eaten the lettuces from his garden.

Then spoke Thoth. 'Let the seed of Horus be revealed upon the brow of Set.' A golden glow emerged from the dark god's head as a sun disc appeared. Set was furious. He would have snatched the sun away and but Thoth took the disc and set it on his own ibis head. Only then did Set depart in anger to his own realm.

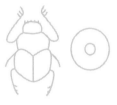

Eighty mortal years had now passed and even Horus had tired of this constant game of war and trickery. He went in person to the ancient Neith who received him at Sais. 'Why has no one thought to ask your father how this matter should be resolved?' she enquired. 'Surely the Lord of the Dead has an opinion which should be considered.' This suggestion was put before Ra who instructed Thoth to write to the underworld for the views of Osiris.

The gods waited impatiently for the reply which took many days. At Ra's behest, Thoth read the letter aloud: 'O Ra, King and first of the gods, I Osiris demand that my son be given the throne of the Two Lands. Why should Horus be cheated of his inheritance? Is it not I who feed mankind and make them strong? Is it not I who makes the barley and the wheat which feed the gods and all living creatures after the gods? Is there any amongst you who can do as I do?'

Hearing this Ra bristled at the impertinence of Osiris and commanded Thoth to set down his reply: 'O Osiris, Benevolent One, Lord of the Dead,' the letter began, 'what if you had never come into existence? Would not the wheat grow? Would the barley wither? I am Ra creator of all and my will is supreme.'

The message was dispatched and many days passed before Osiris's reply was in the hand of Ra. With a little more caution Thoth read aloud: 'O Ra, everything that you have done is good. You are the maker of the nine great gods, but justice in the person of the goddess Maat is with me and it has been so since Set took my throne. What does my presence here mean? I have many emissaries whom I could send to enforce justice on the earth but I do not do this, for did not Ptah tell the very stars that they should rest in the West with me? As indeed will all things. Be realistic O Ra, I am stronger than you and I demand justice for my son or I will be tempted to enforce it.' Ra was silent for a long while as he pondered the words of Osiris.

At length he spoke softly to Thoth. 'This has gone too far, the division between the living and the dead must be maintained. Osiris must not interfere in an affair that concerns the living alone.' Rising to his feet, the sun-god called out the name of Horus. The youth came forward and the mighty Ra solemnly invested him with the Two Crowns, the red and the white, and the Crook and Flail of kingship showing that he was to be Pharaoh over both Upper and Lower Egypt. To Horus came the goddesses Wadjet the cobra of the North, and Nekhebet the vulture of the South to be his protectors for evermore. Then Ra spoke again. 'Let the Lord Set be content for I shall favour him above all others if he will renounce the throne in favour of Horus, son of Isis and Osiris.' From Set there was no answer for the red god had gone far to the south, there to raise the standard of rebellion.

So it was that a flotilla of boats sailed down the sacred Nile to distant Nubia bearing the army of Ra. The sun-god himself took the lead and Horus stood in the prow of Ra's boat and transformed himself into a shining disc with outspread wings, each the colour of the sky at sunset. Then did he cry out to the assembled forces of Set, 'Your eyes shall be blind as he blinded me, your ears shall be deaf as he is to justice.'

At once confusion fell upon the host of Set, for not one man knew his brother or could understand his tongue. And these men were scattered across the earth by Astarte and this is the reason that there are many languages in this world. To cool the fury of Horus, Ra poured a libation of wine and water, which is still done in memory of this battle.

Then Set and his hardened warriors took the forms of crocodiles and hippopotami. In force they charged upriver to overturn the boat of Ra. But Horus was prepared, for his weapon-smiths had provided magical spears and arrows of iron which is known as god-metal. So Horus ordered his forces to let fly their darts and the army of Set was undone. So noble did divine Horus appear that Ra exclaimed, 'Look how Horus casts his weapons against them. He destroys them with his blade. He cuts them into pieces and utterly defeats them.' Six hundred and fifty sorcerous beasts were slain that day, but the ever-wily Set escaped.

To the south-east of Denderah, Horus again sighted his enemy and charged them, carrying devastation to the heart of Set's host. Again Set made his escape but the last battle was not done yet. Now Set made northwards and Horus gave chase.

Set had allies in the marshes of the delta near to his city of Tanis. To these he gave the forms of the beasts of the river. This time he was not so headstrong and he and his forces sank into the mud of the Nile's bed to wait for the boats of Ra to pass overhead.

For four days did Horus and his forces search for their foe. Then on the morning of the fifth day, Set and his demonic allies surfaced and terrible battle was enjoined. Transforming himself into a mighty lion Horus roamed the battlefield like a devouring flame slaying and searching for Set.

Four great battles were fought in the south and four in the north before Set came forward to do combat with Horus. The dust thrown up by their duel was so great that the two were completely obscured from view. All that could be heard were the clash of arms and the shouts of battle. At length Horus staggered from the dust cloud dragging behind him a prisoner who was thrown down before the throne of Ra. 'Look upon Set,' shouted Horus, 'fierce and savage he is, cunning and cruel. His nature is like a beast without kindness or pity. The higher feelings are to him unknown. O Ra, what should be done with the evil one?'

'Take him to Isis, let her decide,' commanded Ra. And so it was done. Isis took the sword of her son and cut off the head of Set, then she dismembered his body and cast its parts far and wide. Thus did Set meet the same fate that had befallen his brother Osiris. However, not all agree that Set was slain in this way but maintain that the final battle has not yet been fought nor will it be until the end of the world when Osiris returns to walk the earth once more.

Then did Horus rule the Two Lands as undoubted Pharaoh and ruled all that was under the light of Ra. And all subsequent pharaohs were hailed as the 'Living Horus'. Peace and plenty were the lot of those who lived during that time for bright Horus returned the lands to the benevolent days of Osiris.

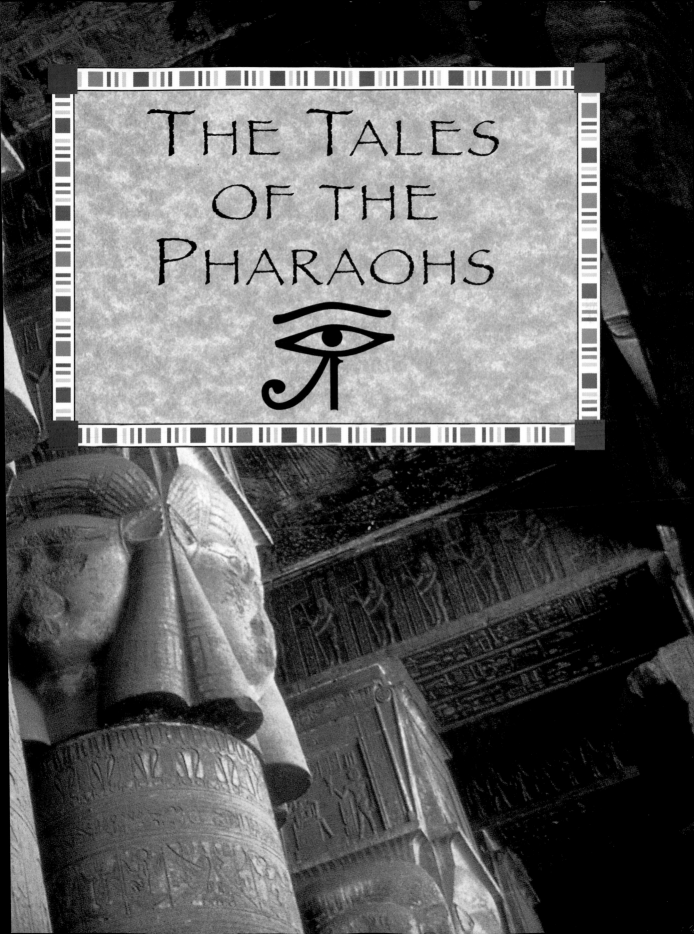

The Tales of the Pharaohs

THE TALES OF THE PHARAOHS

THESE STORIES revolve around those who by fate or, as the Ancient Egyptians would have put it, the will of the gods, had achieved the greatest possible glory: to become Pharaoh of the Two Lands. The use of the word Pharaoh to describe the ruler is something of a misnomer since it is derived from Per-Aa, meaning 'Great House'. This variously represented both the King and the government, and could also describe the huge Karnak temple complex which served as the religious and civil service centre after the Eighteenth Dynasty came to power. Oddly enough the words Per-Aa, which had once described the government of Egypt, eventually developed a different meaning after the time of Alexandra the Great. The Greek invaders corrupted it into 'Pharos', also meaning 'Great House', which refers to the Lighthouse of Alexandria, one of the Seven Wonders of the World.

The first story, 'The Secrets of Thoth', concerns Khufu, a Fourth-Dynasty ruler whose reputation was blackened by subsequent generations. It comes from a papyrus document written about 1800 BC, which is now kept in the Berlin Museum. Its form is that of a folk tale, but the original intent of the story may have been to prove the legitimacy and divine origins of the rulers of the Fifth Dynasty who replaced Khufu's family.

Self-glorification was sometimes the motive behind a story in the mythic style. 'The Cunning General', for example, deals with an officer in the service of Tuthmosis III, the so-called Napoleon of Ancient Egypt. The story formed part of the general's tomb inscription, explaining a commoner's rise to the rank of a nobleman.

It will come as no surprise that Ramesses the Great of the Nineteenth Dynasty, the most powerful and famous of all Egyptian pharaohs, merits a cycle of tales. His seemingly impossible longevity, his many military triumphs, his monument-building, his many marriages and children make him a mythical hero. Later generations told tales, such as 'The Treasury of Ramesses', of his wealth and cunning. This tale comes from Greek historian Herodotus, who referred to the famous king as Rhampsinitis. One of Ramesses' queens, Neferure, features in 'The Princess and the Demon', which was found inscribed on a monumental plaque of the Ptolemaic Period (*c.* 200 BC). This story was used as a propaganda exercise for the superiority of Egyptian knowledge and as a demonstration that it was permissible for a pharaoh to take a foreign wife.

One of the most interesting characters of the Ramesses cycle of stories is his eleventh son Khaemwaset, the High Priest of Ptah. The periodic demise of his elder brothers meant that he eventually became heir to the throne but, like his siblings, he too predeceased his father. A wily magician in folklore, he was also an archaeologist, excavating monuments which were ancient even then. His story is told in 'Khaemwaset and the Mummies' and 'Se-Osiris'.

The final tale comes from the Late Period of Ancient Egypt when the power of the native pharaohs was waning and threats from foreign invaders were becoming more of a problem. 'The Rat of Memphis' is a traditional tale of divine intervention similar in character to an early episode in Homer's *Iliad*; it is also paralleled in medieval legends such as the Pied Piper of Hamelin.

THE SECRETS
OF THOTH

LONG AGO THE GREAT PHARAOH Khufu, the Living Horus, commanded that a feast be held in honour of his divine father who had gone into the western Land of the Dead. So, in the great palace of Heliopolis, the City of the Sun, capital of his kingdom, a banquet was prepared. Khufu further ordered that musicians play, maidens dance and that each one of his three sons tell a tale to entertain the assembled company of the nobles, governors, priests and commanders of the Two Lands of Upper and Lower Egypt.

The first to speak was Prince Chephren. 'I will tell your Majesty of a great marvel that occurred in the reign of your ancestor, King Nebka,' he began. A hush descended on the assembled company as he told the remarkable story of the magical revenge wrought by Uba-aner, High Priest of Ptah, on his beautiful, adulterous wife and her youthful lover. By calling on the names of Ra, Ptah, and Sobek, the dreaded lord of the crocodiles, this sorcerous priest, the wisest man in the Two Lands, caused a fearsome crocodile, no less than seven cubits in length, to seize and consume the young man as he refreshed himself in the lake after one of their passionate assignations. Thus by his powerful magic did Uba-aner take revenge.

The Pharaoh Khufu and his court applauded loudly, for they were all enchanted. Eager to surpass his brother, Prince Baufre rose to his feet. 'My brother Chephren has spoken eloquently of magical arts in the time of King Nebka, but now I will tell a tale of a wonder from the time of your Majesty's own father, King Seneferu.'

Prince Baufre held the noble guests spellbound as he told of how King Seneferu had been cast down by a dreadful melancholy and how the scribe Djada-emankh, as wily as Set and as cunning as Thoth, had been summoned to cure the great King's affliction. The scribe commanded that a magnificent barge be prepared, crewed only by the most beautiful virgins in all the Two Lands and bedecked with fine and costly awnings, to divert the despairing Pharaoh. When one of the lovely maidens lost a priceless jewel in the depths of the lake the Pharaoh's misery only increased. Calm Djada-emankh chanted a powerful spell invoking the name of Hapi, god of the Nile, and of Isis, mother of magic. At once the waters parted to reveal the lost jewel glistening in the mud. By this wonder was the good humour of King Seneferu restored.

King Khufu was pleased with this story and commanded that offerings of incense, beer and loaves be made to the shades of his father and to the marvellous scribe Djada-emankh. Then it was the turn of the King's third son, Prince Hertataf: 'O King, my father, you have heard both my brothers speak of wonders of the past, and

THE PYRAMID KINGS

THE MAIN characters in 'The Secrets of Thoth' date from the Fourth and Fifth Dynasties of Egyptian kings, yet their relationships and personalities are not necessarily historically accurate.

The Pharaoh Khufu (2589–2566 BC) was identified as the builder of the Great Pyramid at Giza by Manetho, the third-century-BC historian of the dynasties, who referred to him as Suphis. Earlier, the Athenian traveller and historian Herodotus had called this king Cheops.

Khufu, Suphis or Cheops was traditionally regarded as contemptuous of the gods, although he is said to have later repented of this impious attitude and provided the Egyptian people with their much-esteemed 'Sacred Books'. Even so, Khufu's reputation was inferior to that of his son Chephren (or Khafra, 2558–2532 BC), or his grandson Menkaure (or Mycerinus, 2532–2504 BC).

Contrary to the story, Khufu was not immediately followed by his son Chephren, nor was Menkaure the last king of the Fourth Dynasty. The first three kings of the Fifth Dynasty were User-ref (2498–2491 BC), Sahu-ra (2491–2477 BC) and Kaku (or Kakai, 2477–2467 BC). However, these three are unlikely to have been brothers and were certainly not triplets.

glorious fictions they are!' Both Chephren and Baufre glared at their younger brother, who continued calmly. 'What man can tell if these are true tales or falsehoods? For there is no one left alive who witnessed these marvels. I alone can vouch for the truth of the tale which I will now relate because its setting is not in the remote past or in a distant land but here within your own kingdom!'

Much to the chagrin of Prince Chephren and Prince Baufre, their father King Khufu leaned forward as he sat upon his exalted throne, more interested now than in the tales of his ancestors. 'Now', continued Hertataf, 'I will tell you of the astounding deeds of a man who lives in our own time!' Far away to the south, yet still within your realm, dwells a man whose prowess at magic is so wondrous that he can raise dead flesh to life again. Even if that flesh has been sliced apart, this sage can restore it to wholeness. He can tame lions and all manner of wild beasts. His home lies in the wilderness at Djedsneferu yet he lacks nothing. His appetites are prodigious since he consumes no less than a thousand loaves of bread a day, drinks no less than a hundred flasks of beer, and, let it be said, physically satisfies the ladies of an extensive harem although he is no less than one hundred and ten years old.

'More than this...' continued Prince Hertataf, 'this sage, whose name is Djedi, has in his possession the secrets of the Sanctum of Thoth, god of wisdom, whose knowledge you need to complete the pyramid so dear to your Majesty's heart.'

'I protest at this nonsense!' cried Prince Chephren.

'And I demand the proof of these claims!' countered Prince Baufre.

Khufu, the King, was astonished, for he had long harboured the ambition of building a pyramid greater than any that had gone before. He was, however, a shrewd ruler, and it needed more than words to win his favour.

'The Princes Chephren and Baufre are right,' remarked the King. 'As you have so boastfully dismissed their tales I command you to equip an expedition at your expense, journey down the sacred Nile and not to dare return without this wonder worker!'

Prince Hertataf bowed low to his stern father. Ignoring the jeers of his elder brothers, and the stunned silence of all the other courtiers he departed from the great palace and equipped a ship, crewed with hardened men. It was long after his ship had passed the last habitations of humanity that Hertataf reached Djedsneferu.

He was carried in a litter to the very doorway of the magician's stately house. Entering, the prince was greeted by the sight of an ancient, wizened man being massaged by servants. The old fellow did not rise or give Hertataf any word of welcome even though it was obvious by his sumptuous clothing and the top-knot upon his head that he was the son of the Pharaoh.

The prince spoke, 'I have come a great distance from the court of my father, the great King Khufu, on a mission that involves the renowned magician Djedi.'

Still there was no hint that the old man had even heard the prince's words.

'I am commanded', continued the prince nervously, 'to convey you to his

Majesty's presence, or else I am to be stripped of my royal status and forbidden to return … if, that is, I am addressing the venerable Djedi?'

The old man stirred upon his couch and, casually waving away his servants, replied simply. 'I am Djedi. I am a person of refined tastes and the prospect of a long voyage up the Nile is not to my liking. Furthermore, I am an old man, being over one hundred and ten years. My time may be short so why should I squander the remainder of my life on the whims of a king, who, as you know, is but the latest in a long line? Kings come and kings go, but there is only one Djedi.'

Prince Hertataf was shocked, not only by the old man's refusal to accompany him, but also at the disrespect shown to his father. In a valiant attempt to sway the old magician, Hertataf spoke more meekly this time. 'O Djedi, if you will come you can be sure that your comforts will be maintained and furthermore that you will be richly rewarded by the king on our arrival at the capital.'

With a show of reluctance, Djedi agreed to go. At next light, a procession of servants carried the magician's books and apparatus to the royal barge.

The magician himself was conveyed to the barge in a litter even more splendid than the prince's own. Once on board Djedi held out his staff, pointing it at his palatial house. Before the prince's eyes it vanished, leaving only wind-blown sand to mark its place. Djedi then directed his staff at the sails which filled with an unseasonable wind, propelling the ship northwards to the court of the King. More swiftly than the prince had thought possible, the ship returned to the city of Heliopolis. The prince at once made for the court of King Khufu. There, he found his father in company with his brothers Chephren and Baufre discussing matters of state.

'Did I not instruct you not to come into my presence again unless you produced your desert wonder worker?' jeered the King. 'Or do you intend to throw yourself upon my mercy and admit your error?'

'Had the error been truly mine, great King, I would freely admit it, but I come with another purpose. I have found the magician Djedi, and even now he is on his way to the palace.'

'This is good news indeed,' cried the King, turning to Chephren and Baufre. 'You see that Hertataf has provided me with a wonder of my own time.'

At this, the palace doors opened to admit the fragile figure of the sorcerer Djedi, who made his way past the princes and scribes to stand before the Pharaoh. Only then did he deign to incline his head in a small bow.

'I have been told that you are the greatest magician in the world,' mused the King, 'yet why is it that before my son spoke of you I had never heard the name of Djedi?'

The magician's voice was like the creaking of an ancient sarcophagus. 'Only they on whom I call, hear my name, O King. Thus I called to your son Prince Hertataf, who spoke of me to you, and came unknowing to fetch me to your presence.'

'My son's words could be considered an outrageous boast on your behalf,' said the King, 'for he claimed that you can raise dead flesh to life again, even if that flesh has been sliced apart. Can you do these things?'

'This I can do,' said Djedi softly.

'Let this toothless boaster make good the claims made for him!' cried Khufu.

A wild duck from the marshes was brought and beheaded before the King and its body was laid at the west end of the hall, while its head was placed to the east. Solemnly Djedi stood between the sundered parts of the bird and, raising his staff, called upon Osiris, lord of the dead and on the goddess Isis, mistress of magic. At once the body and head began to twitch and then to inch towards each other across the great expanse of granite floor. As the two parts reached Djedi's feet he stepped back and body and head were reunited. The magician then clapped his hands, the duck rose and, with a flurry of flapping and squawking, proved without a shadow of doubt that it was truly raised from the dead.

The King was overwhelmed with delight. 'So, the reports of your magic are true,' he enthused, 'but can the same be said of your wisdom? My son Hertataf has told us that you know the secrets of the Sanctum of Thoth which I need to complete the inner chambers of my Great Pyramid. Is this so?'

Djedi smiled. 'It is for this that I called your son to me, and was brought to you O King. It is indeed an irony that the secrets of which you speak are here within the walls of this very city, concealed within a chest of stone.'

'Then I will take possession of them at once,' exclaimed the King.

'No, your Majesty...' said Djedi, 'for it is beyond your power and mine to lay hands on them. The imperishable gods have decreed that only the eldest of the three sons of Rud-Didet may bring them to you.'

'Who is this Rud-Didet?' demanded the King.

'She is the wife of Ra-User, the lord of Sakhebu and High Priest of the sun-god Ra, and she dwells at Leontopolis. But Ra-User is not the father of her sons...' Djedi continued. 'That honour belongs to the sun-god Ra himself, and he has promised that these children shall reign over the Two Lands of Egypt.' At this troubling news King Khufu knew that the favour of the gods was passing from him and his house. 'But out of love for you and your dynasty', Djedi went on, 'Ra has decreed that the eldest son will not come to the throne until both your son and your grandson have reigned after you and passed away, for these infants are not yet born!'

The King sat back upon his exalted throne and was patient for the moment. He called Prince Hertataf forward. 'Let this wise magician be our guest and ensure that he is provided with ample space for his apartments, his servants and his harem. Let one thousand loaves, a hundred bunches of onions, a hundred jars of beer and an ox be given to him each day.'

All was done as the Pharaoh had commanded. The three princes, Chephren, Baufre and Hertataf withdrew from their father's presence in the company of the wise Djedi and the rest of the court, leaving the troubled Khufu to brood on the future as he sat upon the high throne.

In due course Rud-Didet, wife of the lord of Sakhebu, bore three healthy sons. To mark this event a celebration was planned at Leontopolis in the delta. At this time the children's true father, the sun-god Ra, commanded that the goddesses Isis, the lady of magic, Nebhat, Meskhent and Hakt, the overseers of childbirth, disguise themselves as dancing girls to attend the feast. They were to be accompanied by ram-headed Khnum, god of fertility, who would take on the appearance of a porter.

When they arrived the feast was well under way so, taking out tambourines, cymbals and flutes, the disguised goddesses played and danced for Ra-User, his wife Rud-Didet and the assembled guests. As they spun around and around the goddesses sang and in their singing named the three new-born infants User-ref, Sahu-ra and Kaku. They then made their way to the door bidding their host Ra-User to rejoice. Ra-User presented them with a generous sack of barley in payment for their entertainment and the god Khnum placed this sack on his head, following the divine girls into the night.

When they were out of sight of the habitations of men, the goddesses resumed their divine forms. Then Isis said, 'I do not think we should leave without giving the children some token of our godly favour.' Together the four made two crowns by magic: the White Crown of Upper Egypt and the Red Crown of Lower Egypt.

These they gave to Khnum bidding him to conceal the crowns within the barley, return to the house of Ra-User, and there to leave the sack.

Khnum, still in the form of a porter, returned to Ra-User with these words, 'Lord, I carried this sack of barley to the dancing girls as you instructed me, but they are too weak to bear the burden of such a heavy sack and told me to return it to you.'

'I understand perfectly worthy porter,' said Ra-User, 'but it would not do to take back a reward. Place the sack in some cellar, or outhouse. We will keep it safe until such a time when the dancing girls come again.' So Khnum hid the sack in a sealed room of the house and, smiling, departed from Leontopolis.

Some time later Rud-Didet, the mother of the infants, was calculating the household accounts. She enquired of the chief maid if all was in order.

'Yes Madam,' replied the girl, 'except the brewing barley is not yet brought.'

'Why has this not been done?' asked Rud-Didet.

'The barley that was the portion for this house was given to some dancing girls, and it now lies within a locked room,' replied the maid.

Rud-Didet pondered for a moment. 'Open the room and use that barley for the present, and we will replace it when next the dancing girls perform for us.'

The maid took the key and hurried away, but when she entered the room the air was full of the sounds of chariots, of singing, talking and loud fanfares, such as one would hear at the court of the Pharaoh. Frightened, the girl fled back to her mistress.

Rud-Didet then accompanied her servant to the storeroom only to find that the terrified girl had spoken the truth. Here were loud proclamations, invocations to the gods, sounds of feasting and merriment and, not least, the recitations of the titles of the Pharaoh.

Knowing immediately that this was an omen, Rud-Didet opened the sack to reveal the two splendid crowns. Swearing the maid-servant to secrecy, she reverently placed the crowns in a heavy chest, locking it carefully. This chest the two women concealed within another, larger chest, and that in turn within a stone sarcophagus. Each of these was securely locked by Rud-Didet. The noises of the court coming from the crowns were by now so muffled that there would be little likelihood of their discovery.

Some days later, Rud-Didet had occasion to rebuke her maid-servant for carelessness. The disgruntled girl was so angry with her mistress that she made up her mind to go to the Pharaoh Khufu and tell him of the hidden crowns.

She packed a few belongings and set out through the delta towards the distant city of Heliopolis. She had not gone far when she was overcome by a raging thirst. Making her way down to the river's edge she knelt down to drink, whereupon a huge crocodile no less than seven cubits in length rose from the waters and seized her in its terrible jaws, bearing her down into the depths of the water.

When Rud-Didet heard of the maid's doom she knew that her three children were indeed protected by the gods and destined to be kings over the Two Lands.

THE GREAT PYRAMID

THE GREAT PYRAMID of Khufu at Giza is the first and only surviving example of the Seven Wonders of the Ancient World. Originally it was 481 feet in height with sides of 755 feet, each exactly aligned to the four points of the compass. It covers an area of 13 acres and is made up of over 2,300,000 individual blocks of stone. The smallest of these weighs around 2.5 tons.

Until the nineteenth century, it was the tallest man-made structure in the world. Herodotus estimated that the pyramid took twenty years to build, yet estimates for the construction have varied up to several centuries. Herodotus also intimated that, in keeping with his dubious reputation, Khufu put one of his own daughters to work in a brothel to help pay for the building costs.

Professor Piazzi Smyth, the now discredited nineteenth-century Astronomer Royal of Scotland, once calculated that the height of the Great Pyramid was exactly equal to one thousand millionth part of the distance between the earth and the sun, and asserted that its mass was equal to a thousand billionth of the earth's. He also ascertained that the pyramid's base was in direct proportion to the length of the polar axis. Other, more fantastic, claims have also been made for the pyramid – that it is sited on the Giza plateau exactly at the centre of the earth's land surface and has concealed within its dimensions a perfect plan of the universe, mapping out not only the Nile delta, but the extent of the Pharaoh's dominion, the surface area of the planet, and even the height of the moon's orbit.

In recent years, a series of stellar alignments has been proposed for the whole pyramid complex at Giza. The siting of the pyramids does relate to the position of the three stars of Orion's Belt, and the internal shafts of the Pyramid of Khufu line up with the North Star and Great Bear constellation.

If there is any truth in the story of Khufu and his sons, then the sacred scrolls from the Sanctum of Thoth held potent secrets indeed. These secrets now enshrined in the Great Pyramid have not yet been fully uncovered.

THE CUNNING GENERAL

THE PHARAOH TUTHMOSIS III, bearing the banner of his patron god Amun-Ra, gathered his armies and won victories in every land to the north and east, adding to the glory of his name and that of Egypt. He captured cities and took tribute in slaves and gold from their defeated princes. It was during this time of glory and battle that the boldness and resolve of a certain officer named Djehuty came to the attention of the Pharaoh. He was always to be found in the thick of the fighting. Djehuty's courage knew no bounds and his ability to emerge victorious in the face of imminent defeat seemed almost divine. As time went on, this Djehuty was promoted through the ranks of the army until he had attained the high position of general of infantry and military councillor to the King of the Two Lands who thought him the most worthy of his war-lords.

It was at this time that the Prince of Joppa rose in rebellion against the might of Egypt. He slew all the Egyptian soldiers who had been left as garrison within the walls of his maritime city, announcing to the world that his allegiance to the Pharaoh Tuthmosis was over.

This was a dreadful blow to the ambitions of the Pharaoh, for Joppa was a strong city which lay directly on his routes of supply and there was now a serious danger that Tuthmosis and his forces would be trapped without provisions in the north with no chance of escaping back to Egypt. It was this dire problem which occupied the King and his councillors as they sat upon stools in his tent in the wastelands of the Syrian desert.

For some time none spoke as each man there pondered on their perilous position. At length it was Djehuty who broke the gloomy silence. 'Great Tuthmosis,' he began, 'you have in your Majesty's possession a magical staff which has been handed down in your family since the old times. It is said that this staff is a potent talisman blessed by the gods themselves and that he who holds it is granted the power to take become any person or any thing thus becoming invisible or unrecognizable.'

'You speak truly, General,' replied the King, 'but I confess myself puzzled as to the use of such an item in our present troubles.'

'If you will lend me this wondrous staff and equip me with a company of but two hundred men of your Majesty's infantry I will undertake to conquer the rebellious city of Joppa and slay its treacherous prince.' So spoke Djehuty.

The confidence of the general was such that Tuthmosis readily agreed even though the magical staff had been part of the regalia of his house long before they had aspired to the throne of the Two Lands. Unwrapping the relic carefully the Pharaoh solemnly handed it to his general. Conscious of the great trust that had been placed on him Djehuty bowed and departed the tent to take his pick of the Egyptian troops. This task done the general called on craftsmen to prepare a large bag of animal skins, two pairs of fetters, shackles, yokes and many lengths of rope. When all was made ready Djehuty had little else to do but wait for the morning.

As the sun rose on the morrow a party of two hundred men led by the general left the Egyptian camp. The remaining soldiers wondered where these men were bound since they were so oddly equipped. Each departing man led a donkey and upon the back of each beast were two large urns.

Marching swiftly to the west the company reached the sea within three days. They then proceeded southwards towards Joppa. When he was in sight of the city Djehuty ordered his men to make camp while he called on the power of the magical staff to disguise himself as a humble messenger. Then Djehuty made his way into Joppa in the guise of a herald.

The Prince of Joppa for his part was alarmed to see an Egyptian force so close to his city and fully expected this Egyptian herald to demand his immediate surrender: a course of action that the prince was not willing to contemplate having resolved to defend Joppa against Tuthmosis. However, the herald handed the prince a message of different import. Cutting the seal with a small knife the prince read: 'August Prince of Joppa, I am the General Djehuty, famed on the field of battle who has risen through the ranks and given true service to my king. As you may know I was once military councillor to Tuthmosis of Egypt but no longer. For this Tuthmosis has by his base actions proved himself to be a coward and traitor unfit to wear the Double Crown of Egypt. It is with no exaggeration that I say to you plainly that though the Pharaoh raised me up, at length he grew jealous of my prowess in battle, would not listen to my strategies and eventually resolved to do away with me. Had he done this in an honourable fashion I would have accepted my fate, but he plotted to have me poisoned which is an ignoble end. Thus I renounce my allegiance to this Pharaoh and to his house and offer my services and those of my men to you and to the city of Joppa. In token of my good faith I will personally present to you a magical talisman in the form of a staff which was handed down for many centuries through the royal house of Thebes to the Pharaoh which I, by guile, have stolen from him.'

So read Joppa's astonished ruler. He had heard of the fearsome reputation of this Djehuty and knew that he would be a powerful ally in his war against the might of Egypt. Taking up pen and parchment the prince immediately replied accepting the general's offer and promising him all the lands and honours that a prince could provide. This letter the prince handed to the disguised Djehuty who bowed politely and made his way through the thronged streets of the city past the mighty guarded gates and back to the Egyptian encampment.

Within the course of one day, the Prince of Joppa set out from the city gate to meet with Djehuty. He took with him a company of his personal bodyguard, for he was anxious to meet this daring warrior who was to become his new ally. He was equally eager to lay his hands on the magical staff of all-seeing that had been promised to him.

At the Egyptian camp Djehuty, now possessing his true form and the full regalia of a general, welcomed Joppa's ruler and invited him to dine in his humble tent. Though the fare was poor and the comforts sparse, the prince and general showed signs of amity and good humour. Some time passed before the prince broached the subject of the magical staff. 'It pleases me greatly that you have seen the good sense to bring your forces to the city of Joppa, O General,' said the prince smiling, 'but I confess myself anxious to see the wondrous magic of the staff of Tuthmosis which you have promised me.'

'No sooner do you make a wish, O Prince, than it is granted,' replied Djehuty, sending a soldier to fetch the object. Soon the staff lay in the general's hands.

'Is this plain stick the staff you spoke of?' enquired the prince.

'Indeed it is Highness, but to demonstrate its powers fully I must raise it above my head.' So saying, Djehuty raised the staff aloft and, before the Prince of Joppa could so much as shriek, the general brought it down upon his head, felling him senseless, to the ground.

As soon as Djehuty had ensured that he was not overheard by any of the prince's guards he thrust the unconscious ruler into the large skin bag, shackling his hands and feet. Tying the bag carefully, he then called on the power of the staff once more to give himself the shape and appearance of Joppa's prince. Only then did he summon a bodyguard to the tent. Gesturing for silence he whispered, 'See how I have overpowered and bound the treacherous Djehuty whose intent it was to slay me for this is nought but a plot. I will wager that the cowardly Egyptians are fled into the night.' So saying the pair left the tent to find that not a single Egyptian remained in the camp.

The Joppan guard was amazed by his ruler's wisdom and guile in defeating such a resourceful adversary as General Djehuty. 'See those heavily laden donkeys,' said the disguised Djehuty. 'The general told me that they were bearing treasure looted from the northern cities. Go, command my men to lash them together and take them into the city for the booty that once belonged to Tuthmosis will now be mine. I will send a messenger to my wife to tell her that Djehuty is conquered and that she should stand ready to open the gates to receive the body of my vanquished foe and the treasure that I have taken from the Egyptians.'

So it was that a procession set forth from the deserted Egyptian encampment. Djehuty, still disguised as the prince, was at its head with the prince in a sack borne behind him. The guards followed leading a caravan of two hundred donkeys each bearing two great urns upon their backs.

Obedient to her lord's message the prince's chief wife stood upon the strong walls of Joppa until she spied her husband, guards, donkeys and all approaching the gates. At once she commanded that they be opened to admit the procession.

As the great gates closed behind them, Djehuty cried, 'Let us now open these jars which are brimming with treasure and rejoice for victory is ours.' At these words the urns were cut from the backs of the donkeys, shattering upon the ground. From two hundred of the jars leapt two hundred fully armed Egyptian warriors who set upon the stunned defenders of Joppa. Then Djehuty abandoned his disguise and, with his sword, slashed open the sack which held the shackled form of the true prince. 'Surrender, O men of Joppa,' he bellowed, 'or your ruler's head shall be parted from his body.' At these words, the warriors of Joppa fell to their knees and offered up their weapons as tokens of their surrender.

With the yokes of wood and lengths of rope that had been concealed in the other two hundred jars, the soldiers of the Pharaoh bound their captives while Djehuty climbed to the topmost tower of Joppa to raise the ram-headed standard of Amun-Ra, the patron god of Egypt. Then the general sent a message northwards to the encampment of Pharaoh with these words: 'Lord of the Two lands, I have captured the Prince of Joppa and all the people of Joppa are my prisoners. Let them be sent for and brought into the land of Egypt, that your house may be filled with male and female slaves who will be yours for ever. Let Amun-Ra, thy father, the god of gods be glorified forever.'

When the Pharaoh Tuthmosis read these words and was told of the details of this bloodless victory he praised the ingenuity of his most cunning general and granted him the titles and lands befitting a noble of the Two Lands. Thus did Djehuty prosper until the end of his days.

THE TREASURY OF RAMESSES

HE MIGHTY PHARAOH, Ramesses the Great, relentlessly led his armies into battle to conquer vast territories and lay claim to tribute from the many cities that he subjugated. He was not a ruler who was content to wear the Red and White Crowns of peaceful dominion; he had driven his chariot into the thick of battle, charging his enemies and grinding their forces into the dust. For Ramesses, the favoured royal headgear was the Blue Crown of War. His reputation was daily enhanced by the arrival of sumptuous treasures from all corners of his mighty empire which stretched from the lonely wastes deep in the heart of Libya, to the deserts of Syria. These offerings were ferried down the Nile to his capital, Thebes of the Hundred Gates, the greatest city on the face of the earth.

The kings of the world fawned at his feet and tried to curry favour with the mighty ruler by bringing the most rare and wonderful gifts to please him: ivory from the unknown lands of Africa, spices, unguents, gorgeous fabrics and gold from Assyria, Medea and even the distant plains of Asia. The treasures of Nubia, Ethiopia, Libya, Phoenicia, Judea and Edom were laid at his feet as he sat aloof upon the Horus Throne, clutching the Crook and Flail of rulership to his chest and wearing upon his head the awesome Double Crown of Upper and Lower Egypt which proclaimed him to be the Son of the Sun and the true earthly master of the world.

Ramesses adorned the length of the Nile with temples and palaces. Huge colossi reared

above the blue waters of the sacred river as Ramesses glorified his own name as well as those of his gods. But even as he lavished the riches that came into his grasp on these ambitious projects, more still flowed from the subject lands to fill his coffers.

The Pharaoh soon realized that no matter how much he expended on wars and building projects, his resources were infinite. He therefore decided to build a vast treasury to contain his awesome wealth which, in time, would share the eternity of the tomb with him. So Ramesses summoned Paser, the most famous architect in Egypt, to his court and privately instructed him to make a plan of the most cunning and tortuous labyrinth he could devise.

The architect began work at once and the cunning structure rose from the desert near Thebes as the labourers worked night and day to fulfil the desires of the King. Paser the architect, too, stretched his imagination and his muscles as he devised ever more ingenious feints and man-traps for his master's labyrinth. At the time of each full moon, soldiers would arrive at the camp to blindfold each and every one of the workmen. Then, Ramesses himself would come, secretly, disguised as a common man. Together with his architect, the King would pace out the way through the maze again and again until he had every twist, turn, pitfall and deadly puzzle perfectly consigned to memory.

When the building was ready the vast treasure hoard was placed inside. As the last labourer vanished into the interior gloom of the maze, Ramesses ordered his warriors to take up their arms and wait by the huge portal. To the architect's horror, as each of the labourers emerged unburdened he was struck down by soldiers, until not one man was left alive.

'Thus does Ramesses the King keep his secrets,' murmured the Pharaoh.

Having witnessed these events, Paser felt terrified. Was he to meet the same fate as the poor workmen? Throwing himself before the King he stammered, 'Oh Lord of All the Lands, I know the way to the centre of this structure better than anyone. Is my fate to be sealed in the same manner as my servants?'

'Be of good cheer,' replied Ramesses coldly, 'for it is necessary that one man remain alive who knows the secret, for not even I will live for ever and my heir must be initiated into the mysteries of this place by someone. You have kept faith with me, and I will now do likewise with you … After all, I may have need of your architectural services again for I am not a wasteful man. Return to your home. You will be rewarded for the service that you have done for me.'

Shaken to the core, the poor man bowed and left the gloating Ramesses to contemplate his treasure store. He quickly made his way back to Thebes for nothing could comfort him now except the loving embrace of his wife and sons.

'Ramesses is not the only man who has sons and heirs,' he muttered to himself.

Retiring to his bed, Paser realized that his days would be few. He therefore called his two beloved sons to his bedside. 'My dear children,' he began, 'you know that

RAMESSES THE GREAT

ANY DESCRIPTION of the Nineteenth-Dynasty Pharaoh Ramesses II (*d.* 1212 BC) so easily becomes a list of superlatives. He built the greatest monuments, achieved the most victories and extended Ancient Egyptian dominion to its farthest extent. He had 13 heirs, including Khaemwaset, 12 of whom predeceased him, as did at least 26 of his other children. His reign of 67 years was only surpassed by Pepi II of the Sixth Dynasty (*d.* 2184 BC) who allegedly ruled for 94 years from the age of four.

A tomb in the Valley of the Kings, originally intended for Ramesses, now known as KV5 and previously thought to be of little interest, has been discovered to be the largest in the Theban Necropolis. It is a veritable maze, with many side-chambers, levels and passageways. This tomb was not used for the King but provided a sepulchre for many of his sons.

When Ramesses passed beyond the Gates of Night it must have seemed that one of the eternal gods had died, if only because he had reigned for more than two average human lifespans at that time. The mighty Pharaoh was laid to rest in Tomb 7 (KV7) of the Valley of the Kings, but his instantly recognizable hawk-nosed mummy can now be found in the Cairo Museum.

for many years I have served the Pharaoh Ramesses, and that the service I have given him, and the pains that I have endured in his name have shortened my life.' The boys protested that their father had yet many years before him. 'Not so, for already I hear the call of the jackal-god Anubis calling me to the tomb. But before I make that last, final journey I will share a secret with you both; a secret so deadly that were the King to hear of it he would immediately end your lives.'

The architect lifted himself painfully from his bed and continued his tale. 'In the desert not far from this great city is a mighty building, the construction of which has robbed me of my health, my ingenuity and my faith. I have seen good friends die for the greed of Ramesses and I now would have my payment for the terrible miseries I have endured. The King's greatest treasures lie within those impregnable walls. Beyond its thick doors is a maze from which the most clever of thieves would have no hope of escaping alive. But there is one thing that even the King does not know: I created another secret entrance to the building, a single stone which may be split into two by a cunning mechanism of my own devising. One man may do this with difficulty but two men may do it with ease, if they know how.' Paser paused for breath. 'Anyone who enters the building by this way may safely pass through the labyrinth to the treasure store, there to take his pick of the choice goods which lie within. I will teach you both the secret of the stone and the pathway through the maze so that I may die happy in knowledge that my family will prosper at the expense of a cruel king.'

With that, the architect rose unsteadily to his feet and, stumbling, trod out the pathway that his sons must take. Again and again he paced the earthen floor until both young men could follow his footfalls step by step. Now, satisfied that they had learnt the lesson well and would not forget, the architect sank back on to his humble bed and breathed his last dying breath.

Stricken with grief, the elder son Paweraa sent for the embalmers to mummify the remains of his father, while the younger tried to comfort his distraught mother. Later that day, the younger brother said, 'Let us go to the treasury at once and steal some gold to give our father a sumptuous funeral.'

The elder reacted with anger. 'That would give our secret away at once, and that is not what our father would have wanted. Let us wait a while and then we will tread the labyrinth together to see what may be seen.' To this the younger acquiesced even though he was impatient to rob the treasury of the King.

The seventy days of mourning elapsed and Paser's mummy was laid to rest in a small rocky tomb on the western shore of the Nile. 'Now,' whispered the younger brother to the elder, 'it is a good time to enter the treasury. I know that you will have some clever argument against this, but I say that we have the perfect opportunity for is not our father entombed, and Ramesses far away with his armies?'

After many hushed words between them the younger brother had his way so, at dead of night guided by the dim light of the moon, the pair made their way through the desert to the treasury. Following their father's instructions they paced around the walls until they came to a stone which was of a slightly different texture to the others. Muttering a prayer to Anubis, the opener of ways, the elder brother Paweraa placed his hand upon the right-hand portion of the stone while the younger placed his upon the left. Pushing, the two were overjoyed to see the stone part revealing the dark interior. Crawling through the gap they pushed the stone from within until it closed seamlessly. Only when no sliver of moonlight remained from the outside did the brothers light a lamp. Carefully, paying attention to each footfall, they moved through the gloom, the light from the lamp casting eerie shadows about them. Here, they must walk on the left-hand side of the passageway, there they must crawl, and at another place they walked singly lest their combined weight tip the delicate balance that would plunge them to their doom. At length they arrived at the inner chamber and were astounded by the mound of fabulous riches that met their eyes.

'Brother,' whispered the younger, 'let us take as much as we can from this place and we will live like kings.'

'No,' countered Paweraa. 'We have here a store of wealth that will last us for many years, but if we take too much Ramesses will notice the loss upon his return and hunt us down. Choose some small but expensive items that are easily carried from the back of the hoard and be satisfied with the bounty that our father has given us.'

Grumbling, the young brother did as he was told. The elder assured himself that they had left no evidence of their presence and they then made their departure, taking as much care on the way out as they had on the way in.

So it went at every full moon. The pair would secretly enter the labyrinth, tread its tortuous paths warily and emerge with only small items of value whose loss the King would not notice. The brothers and their mother moved from the small house, in which they had spent their lives, into a larger, more palatial villa. They now had slaves to wait upon them and more wealth than they could spend.

In time, Ramesses the Great, King of Upper and Lower Egypt, the Lord of All the Lands, returned in triumph to his capital Thebes of the Hundred Gates. Loudly the trumpets of war announced the arrival of the King. The people cheered and threw garlands before his chariot and made such a tumult that the noise could be heard far beyond the city walls.

Paweraa, the elder of the architect's sons, listened to the jubilant sounds and realized that the forays into the treasury would have to stop because the risk of discovery now was very great. 'However,' he murmured to himself, 'we have wealth enough and the spirit of our father is sure to be satisfied with what we have gained at Ramesses' expense.'

The younger brother, too, listened to the tumult that issued forth from Thebes. His mind though followed a different course. 'Soon the King will go to the treasury, and who knows what new gems, necklaces and diadems he will deposit there? I for one will find out and make off with the most precious thing that he has gained. Only thus will our father's spirit be satisfied.'

Now it happened that amidst Ramesses' booty was a particularly beautiful pectoral ornament shaped into a likeness of the Eye of Horus. The King made his way to the treasury, opened the great doors and carefully wound his way to the heart of this most secure of repositories. Pausing to gloat over his immense wealth, he placed the eye in a prominent position so that he could gaze upon its beauty every time he entered the central chamber. Satisfied, he trod the secret ways back to the outside world.

Not long after the King had made his departure another arrived at the walls of the treasury. This was the younger brother who had observed Ramesses and knew by the King's rapt expression that something truly wondrous had been concealed within. With some difficulty the young man parted the two halves of the stone and, with an assurance born of habit, passed through the labyrinth. There, in the inner chamber which was piled so high with riches of all description, he was entranced by the startling loveliness of the King's newest acquisition and fell in love with it. 'Oh lovely jewel,' he groaned, 'I must possess your beauty.' So saying, he seized it and ran back through the maze.

The young man was so captivated by his find that he did not pay sufficient attention to his steps as he dashed for the hidden exit. All at once, a section of the wall surged forward as a mighty block of stone was propelled outwards with enormous force. The architect's youngest son screamed as the block caught him and crushed him against the opposite wall. The gleaming Eye of Horus fell from his numbed hand as the boy hung there dying, his blood pooling about his mangled legs.

Paweraa, meanwhile, had noticed the absence of his brother and, fearing the worst, made haste to the treasury. After ensuring that he was alone and unobserved he approached the secret portal with dread for he saw that it was still open and knew that his foolish brother was inside. Entering on his hands and knees his fingers encountered a sticky wetness on the floor. Trembling, Paweraa fumbled with his lamp. As the light flared he was horrified to see the ghastly vision of the poor crushed body of his brother still pinned to the wall by the stone. Even worse than this was the fact that he still lived: his eyes silently pleading with his elder brother to put him out of his torment.

Paweraa, now stained with blood, cradled the younger's face. 'You must end this,' croaked the boy. 'Cut off my head so that Ramesses will not be able to identify me, for if he does your life will be forfeit too.' Though shocked by his grisly discovery, Paweraa knew that his sibling was beyond help. He kissed the boy while drawing a long curved knife from his belt. Then, still holding his brother's eyes with his own, he sliced through his brother's neck, ending his intolerable pain.

Wrapping the bloody relic in his cloak, the sobbing Paweraa crawled from the treasury. There was no need to close the secret entrance now for soon the King would know all. All, that is, except the identity of those who had robbed him. Stricken with grief and guilt for the terrible thing that he had been forced to do, the architect's remaining son made his unsteady way to his home.

The next day Ramesses the King again went to his treasury eager to feast his eyes on his newest spoils. Again the vault was opened and he trod the pathways with great care, but when he opened the inner chamber he immediately discovered the theft of the Eye of Horus. Roaring with rage he overturned jewel cases and jars of precious stones. It was then that he realized that other, smaller items had also been stolen from this the strongest refuge that the mind of man could devise.

'No man save I knows the secret way to this place,' muttered the King, 'therefore there must be another hidden entrance.' With these words the King retraced his steps to rejoin his guards without.

Emerging, Ramesses commanded that a thorough search be made of the outside of the treasury and it was not long before one of his guards raised an alarm. Hastening to the spot the King spied the sundered stone, observed the mark of a bloodstained hand and the golden glint of his abandoned jewel, now resting in a pool of gore. Within, of course, was the headless corpse.

'Take this piece of carrion and impale it outside the Royal Gate of Thebes,' thundered the King, 'for he was not alone in this enterprise, and it is in my mind to catch his accomplice and put him to a similar end.'

So, the carcass of the foolish younger brother was raised high on a pole at the Royal Gate of Thebes and soldiers set to guard it. Ramesses commanded that note be taken of any who paused at the corpse, and that if any cried out or showed grief in any other way, they should be seized and brought to him at once.

Paweraa soon heard of the mysterious corpse raised high at the gate and, knowing that it was the body of his own dear brother, resolved to steal it so it could be reunited with its head and entombed with their father in proper fashion. Without delay he saddled some asses and loaded them with goatskins full of expensive wine. He then put on the garb of a merchant and led the animals to the city. Taking care that he did not so much as glance upwards at the body of his brother, the thief made small incisions in some of the goatskins. Whistling, he led the asses passed the guards. As he did so, the wine splashed against a soldier's bare leg.

As the soldier protested at the lost wine, the cunning thief then made such an outcry that all the guards rushed about to grasp any container that could save the precious liquid. Even so, much was lost upon the ground. 'Let us lie on the ground and catch the wine in our mouths,' shouted the first guard. At this the soldiers at once began to gulp down the wine as it fell from the goatskins. The disguised Paweraa put his arm around the commander and offered to exchange one of the remaining skins of wine for some meat. This the officer readily agreed to and soon yet another goatskin was breached.

Night had now fallen and, one by one, the soldiers fell into a drunken sleep. The thief, still in merchant's garb, clambered up the impaling pole to cut down his brother's body. Concealing it within one of the empty wine skins, Paweraa devised a way to teach the feckless guards a lesson and to insult King Ramesses into the bargain. Taking out his curved knife, the very same with which he had decapitated his brother, he shaved off half the beards of each and every one of the sleeping soldiers. This done he fled into the night, chuckling at his ingenuity.

When King Ramesses heard of this trick he was furious and swore that he would use any means at his disposal to find the culprit. Yet he could think of no stratagem that would lure this cunning and elusive thief into the open. At length his daughter, the Princess Bintanath, came to Ramesses with a plan of her own.

So it was that the Princess Bintanath stood between the pylons of the Temple of Amun and was stripped of her royal name and titles. Before a stunned and silent throng her coronet was taken from her head and her bracelets from her wrists. Now disgraced, she was escorted to a low area of the city there to be installed in a common brothel to ply what trade she might. However, Ramesses had ordered that guards in disguise attend her wherever she went to ensure that she came to no harm.

The news was put abroad that the daughter of the Pharaoh was selling her body. To each the fallen princess asked, 'What is the cleverest and wickedest thing that you have ever done?' Each man told his tale, and each was immediately dismissed from her presence when it became evident that he was not the thief she sought.

Paweraa, in the mean time, had buried the body of his brother and performed the seventy lawful days of mourning when he heard that Bintanath, daughter to King

Ramesses, was a harlot in the city. At this news he smiled and, just as the princess had predicted, he counted the ways in which he had discomfited the King. 'First I stole gems and gold from Ramesses, and that was a portion of his treasure; then I stole the remains of my brother from his clutches, and that was a portion of his honour; now I will steal a night of love with his daughter and that will be a portion of his shame.' So saying, he bathed and dressed himself in his finest garments, fitting raiment to pay a visit on even a fallen princess.

On his way to the city the clever thief Paweraa fell prey to suspicion and, fearing a trap, cut the arm off a body that lay exposed on the wayside. This cold member he concealed beneath his richly brocaded cloak. At length he came to the bawdy house that was the present home of Bintanath. At the door he was accosted by a Nubian slave who asked him his business, then ushered him into the presence of the beautiful daughter of Ramesses.

At once, Paweraa was overcome with passion but she retreated saying, 'You have sworn to abide by my conditions, Sir; you must first tell me your name.'

'My name is Paweraa, son of Paser the architect,' he replied, moving closer.

'Now tell me of the wickedest thing that you have ever done,' purred the princess.

'I cut off the head of my own brother,' groaned the thief.

'Oh evil man,' she teased seductively, 'now tell me of your cleverest escapade.'

'I stole my brother's body from the soldiers of your own father by making them drunk and then shaving off half of their beards,' replied Paweraa with some pride.

'Then you are the very man for me,' cooed the princess as she enfolded him in her arms kissing him passionately. However, this was but a ploy for she seized his arm and called out. The guards who had been hidden behind the rich hangings of the room leapt out to capture the cunning thief, but Paweraa, more cunning than the princess, easily slipped from her grasp for she held on to nothing more than the dismembered arm of the wayside corpse. With a mocking laugh Paweraa fled through the window and into the night.

Her wiles defeated, the princess returned to her father confessing Paweraa to be the most subtle and cunning man that she had ever known. However, the surprises of the night were not yet over for within the hour the King's thoughts were disturbed by the arrival of the thief himself who humbly presented himself before the Horus Throne.

'You are either the bravest man in my many kingdoms, or the most foolish, Paweraa,' said the King.

'Your Majesty, I have come to throw myself on your mercy, for I know that there is nowhere in the world that I could hide from your wrath now that you know my identity. I have therefore come to accept whatever punishment you see fit to inflict upon me, but I plead for my mother who had no part in my crimes.'

The Great Ramesses was silent for a short while before speaking. 'Paweraa, cunning thief, son of my architect Paser, I condemn you to a fate so terrible that you will bear its awful burden for the rest of your days.' By now Paweraa's nerve was failing and he began to tremble. Ramesses continued, 'I condemn you to be my chief minister within the city of Thebes and to ensure that the law is upheld from now until the day you die.'

Astonished, Paweraa stole a glance at the figure on the throne. 'But, Majesty ...'

Ramesses laughed. 'Anyone who can get the better of me on not one but three occasions is a person to be reckoned with, and one who can be used. As I once informed your father, I am not a wasteful man.'

The King then decreed that Paweraa and Bintanath should be married and that they administer the city of Thebes of the Hundred Gates under his rule, for Ramesses admired the cunning thief who had so outwitted him, especially since he considered himself to be the most astute of men.

THE PRINCESS AND THE DEMON

RAMESSES THE GREAT, Pharaoh of the Two Lands of Egypt, monarch of the cities of Phoenicia, Canaan and Syria, and over-lord of many others, was unsurpassed in battle. As his long reign progressed, ever more lands came under his vast dominion until at last he was the most powerful ruler in the world. He seemed a living god to be worshipped by his many subjects.

Each year the subjects of the Pharaoh gathered at the town of Nahairana, at the mouth of the River Euphrates, to pay homage to Ramesses. Many lesser kings and princes vied with each other by making gifts to Ramesses to win his royal favour. Gold, jewels, turquoise and lapis lazuli, precious wood, incense and stone carvings there were in plentiful abundance, but also there were the maidens of royal blood, brought to Nahairana to please the Great Pharaoh and to enter his extensive harem.

Among the petty princes who attended this gathering was the ruler of Bakhtan, far to the north. As the king of that mountainous region he wished to win the support of Ramesses against the might of the Hatti, who constantly threatened his borders. With this in mind he wondered what present would be worthy of the Pharaoh of Egypt since Bakhtan was a poor country with no gold or jewels to offer.

The King of Bakhtan bowed low before Ramesses, Pharaoh of Egypt and Lord of All the Lands. Grovelling in the dust before the throne, the ruler of the mountains explained that he was a poor man and could not afford to equal the gorgeous gifts that other, more prosperous, lands had rendered as tribute. Then it came to him that Bakhtan did indeed possess two jewels: his twin daughters who shone like the sun and the moon. 'Surely,' thought the penurious King, 'the mighty Ramesses will instantly fall in love with one of these, though I cannot bear to send both to faraway Egypt or my heart would break.'

Gathering his courage the poor King spoke aloud, 'O Pharaoh, if I may be allowed to return to my country I will send you a jewel that is unsurpassed.'

The great Ramesses waved him away, unimpressed by this unlikely promise.

So it was that the king of the impoverished country of Bakhtan returned to his mountainous home intent on sending Ramesses his eldest daughter. When the two princesses heard of their father's decision they were inconsolable because it meant that they would be separated for ever. The eldest, whose fate it was to be sent to the land of the Nile, tearful herself, told her sister Bentresh to take heart and to send a message if anything was ever amiss, for then she would prevail on her husband to send all the help that he could. Sobbing still, she then entered the paltry litter that had been prepared for her and with but one elderly servant and a guard of no more than two rough mountain men set off for the distant land of Egypt and the court of the mightiest ruler in the world.

The journey was arduous and beset with hardships. First there were the mountains themselves, the cold and treacherous passes which had to be traversed before the party could reach the warmer more southerly lands. Then there were the harsh wastelands of sand and rock where no water flowed; in these places the princess devoutly wished to return to her cool, wet homeland. More than once did her guards beat off the attacks of ill-disciplined bandits, and all began to doubt that they would live to see the land of the pyramids. However, after the moon had waxed and waned more than eight times, the small party came to a city garrisoned by Egyptian troops. When all was explained the city commander rewarded the two guards and sent them back to their wild home. The princess herself was housed in the best quarters in the city while arrangements were made to convey her in more comfort and safety to the presence of the Pharaoh.

The moon waxed and waned four more times and it was the twenty-second day of the second summer month before the Princess of Bakhtan arrived in Thebes of the Hundred Gates. The city was jubilant, not for the arrival of this princess from an obscure far-off land, but for the Opet festival which marked the annual flooding of the sacred Nile and when the holy boat of the god Amun-Ra was held aloft for all to see. Hesitantly, the princess was led through seemingly endless halls and corridors eventually to stand

before the exalted throne of Ramesses. In all her long journey she had dreamed of Ramesses. What was he like? Was he youthful or aged? Vigorous or decrepit? But even now as she stood in his presence she could not bear to raise her eyes to gaze upon him.

Now Ramesses was in the twenty-second year of his reign and was not as youthful as the hero of the princess's imagination. Nevertheless, when she gained enough courage to look upon him she instantly fell in love. Ramesses for his part was intrigued by this new acquisition for his harem and commanded that she let fall her veil and stand before him naked. Trembling, the girl loosed the fastenings and allowed her garment to fall to the polished floor.

Ramesses the King was astonished by the radiant beauty of this barbaric princess which illuminated the high-ceilinged hall of audience. 'In all my life I have never beheld such loveliness,' said the Pharaoh. 'In all the world there can be nothing to compare with the beauty of the Princess of Bakhtan. I swear that I will take her as a wife and set her above all my other concubines.'

The scribes of the court hurriedly set down the Pharaoh's words as he stepped down from the throne reverently to place her fallen gown again upon her shoulders. 'From this day forth let this princess be known as Neferure which signifies the Beauty of Ra, for no earthly thing is a fit comparison for her divine loveliness.' With these words Ramesses the Great, Lord of All the Lands married the Princess of Bakhtan and proclaimed her Great Royal Wife, second only to him in supremacy. With much ceremony the priests of Karnak set the Vulture Crown of Egyptian queens upon her brow and all the secondary wives of the Pharaoh, his many children and all the priests, scribes and functionaries of the court did her homage before she was presented before the people who likewise did her honour and rejoiced.

A year passed in peace and prosperity for all the people of the empire of Ramesses. The Pharaoh was content to spend his days in the company of his lovely wife, and she was content to be with him save for an occasional longing for the company of her beloved sister Bentresh. Again the Opet festival came to pass and the holy boat of Amun-Ra was taken from his shrine in the vast temple of Karnak for all the people to see. It was through this joyous confusion that a bedraggled messenger pushed his way to the royal palace. Long did he argue with the guards at the gate until eventually he was taken to the eunuch servants of the Pharaoh, these in turn conveyed

the miserable messenger to the chief butler, who after lengthy persuasion brought him to the minister of the city. This worthy lord, a son-in-law of the King who was rumoured to have once been a notorious thief, eventually brought the weary fellow to the garden pavilion in which the Pharaoh Ramesses and the Great Royal Wife Neferure took their ease.

Prostrating himself before them the messenger spoke, 'Great King and glorious Queen I have journeyed for many a month from the land of Her Majesty's birth to bring dire news and to request assistance, for already I may have failed in my mission due to the time it has taken me to come into your august presences.'

Realizing that the bedraggled man spoke in the accents of Bakhtan, Queen Neferure raised him to his feet and gave him wine from her own cup. Gasping, he continued, 'As your Majesty knows it is a perilous journey from the mountains of the far north to the blessed realm of Ramesses, and I have lost all my companions along the weary way. Soon though I must return with or without the boon that my master requires.'

Then the Great Ramesses spoke, 'Tell us your tale swiftly, for only then can we render assistance.'

The messenger continued, 'Sadly it is a woeful one concerning the Queen's sister Bentresh, who from the day Neferure departed from Bakhtan pined and wept for her loss. The King, her father, tried every remedy to cure his daughter's melancholy but to no avail and soon it became evident by various tokens that a wild demon of the mountains had inhabited her body and cursed the land. As she wailed and thrashed for day after day, month after month, the crops withered and the cattle died. The King of Bakhtan was beside himself with anxiety so he called on magicians and priests from far and wide to effect the cure of his daughter but none has met with success. Thus, in desperation, he has sent me to implore the help of the skilled physicians of Egypt to save our poor, small kingdom and our suffering princess.'

At once King Ramesses sent for the best doctor in the kingdom: a skilled man by the name of Tehuti-em-heb who was famed throughout the world as a master of diagnosis, treatment and the fabled arts of magic. It was he who understood the mysteries of the body and the mind. Swift horses were tethered to chariots and the pair, messenger and physician, immediately set off bound for Bakhtan.

Pausing for neither day nor night their journey was made swifter by the exchange of their beasts at every Egyptian garrison along the way. Even so, it took some months to come to the stricken kingdom. Arriving at the small fortress which served as palace to Bakhtan's kings, Tehuti-em-heb immediately entered the princess's bedchamber. There he found the unfortunate girl thrashing and writhing upon her bed. Setting braziers of sweet-smelling herbs about the bed Tehuti-em-heb raised his wand calling on his magical powers to send his Ka to do battle with the evil demon who had possessed her.

The black soul of the demon oozed forth from the girl and beset the soul of the magician. All through the night the two contended raging this way and that but not once did Tehuti-em-heb have the slightest chance of expelling the foul entity. Eventually beaten and exhausted near to death Tehuti-em-heb fled the room as the monstrous being again took possession of the body of Bentresh.

The King of Bakhtan who had, throughout the spiritual battle, stood shaking at the bedchamber door hastened to the fallen magician's aid. His heart was broken for he now thought that the last hope to save his country and his daughter had gone. Gasping for air Tehuti-em-heb comforted him. 'I will not cease my efforts but it is my belief that I can only limit the evil of the demon and not banish it utterly. Send another messenger to the Pharaoh, for the cure of this affliction is beyond the powers of mortals and belongs to the realm of the gods. Only the Great Ones can now end this terrible curse.'

So it was that another messenger departed from Bakhtan braving the many perils that beset the way. So terrible was this journey that it took one year and five months to reach the court of Ramesses at Thebes.

Miserable and exhausted, this messenger related his sorry tidings before the

Pharaoh and his queen. Weeping, Queen Neferure lifted the man's face between her gentle hands, saying, 'Since I have resided at Thebes I have worshipped at the Temple of the moon-god Khonsu. I have made many sacrifices at his altar and adored him, perhaps he of the lunar disc will grant divine assistance to my beloved sister and to our homeland.'

With much ceremony the Pharaoh Ramesses made his way to the sanctuary of the moon-god Khonsu, son of Amun-Ra. Passing down the grand avenue of the ram-headed sphinxes he entered the holy enclosure of the mighty temple of Karnak. Putting aside his crown the Pharaoh purified himself with holy water and garments which had never before been worn. Only then did he pass from the bright sunshine of the huge courtyard into the shaded interior of Khonsu's shrine. With a deliberation born of many years of practice Ramesses poured the offering libation at the altar of the god and spoke the ritual prayers. As his words echoed about the gloomy shrine the voice of the god rose to greet him.

'My brother Ramesses, beloved of our father Amun-Ra, I Khonsu greet you and know of the boon which you crave of me.'

Even though the Pharaoh had spoken with the gods on many previous occasions, the thrill of another such contact chilled him. 'Mighty god, will you then send divine aid to Bakhtan to cure the suffering Princess Bentresh?' enquired the King.

'That I will,' replied the god, 'but first bring to this temple the image of another aspect of my being. Bring the image of Khonsu the Contriver that I may impart a portion of my own essence into the statue. Then let it be sent to Bakhtan to do battle with the demon.'

With profuse thanks the Pharaoh Ramesses took his leave of the moon-god and commanded that the statue of Khonsu the Contriver in the form of a hawk be brought to the great temple to partake of the power of the son of Amun-Ra. The moon waxed to its fullness as the image absorbed the essence of its mightier twin. Only then was it swiftly conveyed from the city eager to confront the demon in far Bakhtan. The journey again took one year and five months until the procession of Egyptian priests and warriors who accompanied the god arrived at the fortress which served as palace to Bakhtan's king. There at the gate the poor king of this stricken land did homage to the god who had come so far to help him.

Chanting spells, the priests of Egypt brought the hawk form of Khonsu into the bedchamber of the Princess Bentresh. Incense was burned and the holy men took up their stations about the bed as Bentresh thrashed and writhed, her body soaked with sweat. Then the physician Tehuti-em-heb, who had battled the demon constantly for nearly three years, called forth the mighty Ka of Khonsu from the image. Rising into the air the hawk-god challenged the mountain demon which issued forth from the stricken body of the princess in an oily, black cloud. At once the light of the holy moon penetrated the foul darkness causing the possessing entity to shriek with pain

HATSHEPSUT

Q UEEN HATSHEPSUT (*d.* 1458 BC) or rather 'King' Hatshepsut, daughter of the Pharaoh Tuthmosis I of the Eighteenth Dynasty, was originally married to her half-brother, the short-lived Tuthmosis II. After his death she found herself acting as regent for her infant nephew. Realizing that the only bar to assuming the throne was her gender she simply declared herself a man and reigned for twenty years, becoming the world's first, and possibly only, female king.

To legitimize her assumption of the crown, Hatshepsut added the tallest obelisks to the Great Temple of Karnak, and built a beautiful mortuary temple in Western Thebes. She relied heavily on the support of her steward, a commoner rumoured to be her lover. His power was resented especially by the now youthful prince who was to become Tuthmosis III, and who mutilated Hatshepsut's monuments after her demise in an effort to erase her name from history.

In view of Tuthmosis III's actions it is not surprising that the exact location of her tomb is a source of controversy; the tomb dug for the 'King' was found to be empty. The most probable location is within Tomb 60 of the Valley of the Kings (KV60). This sepulchre was considered to be the tomb of the royal nurse Sitre, however, the positioning of the female mummy suggests the royal burial of an unidentified Eighteenth-Dynasty queen. The mummy measures five feet in length, with painted nails and hennaed hair. Further examination revealed that she was elderly, with arthritis in the left knee. Most intriguingly of all, this lady possessed a mask which was originally jewelled, and had a niche at the chin for an angular beard which was only worn by a reigning monarch rather than a consort. Therefore, despite lack of documentary evidence, tomb KV60 is the most likely resting place for the glorious Hatshepsut.

and rage. Again and again did the demon assault the hawk-god only to be wounded and beaten back until at last the inky cloud resolved itself into the demon's true form of a hunched dwarf who prostrated himself before the sacred image. 'Be welcome great Khonsu,' whimpered the dwarf, 'great god who defeats evil spirits. Bakhtan is now your kingdom and all its people are your slaves just as I am your slave. By your leave I will now depart to fulfil your desire.' So spoke the demon.

Khonsu the Contriver replied, 'Be gone at once foul demon and afflict this land no more. Yet, I will command that the King of Bakhtan hold a festival of remembrance and give offerings to you to indicate that I am as magnanimous to a fallen enemy as I am mighty.'

Hearing these words, the King of Bakhtan was overjoyed and commanded that the god's desires be fulfilled at once. He then embraced his daughter, now well once more, and further ordered that Khonsu the Contriver should be exalted above all other gods within his kingdom.

It was during the joyous celebrations for Bentresh's recovery that the King conceived an impious idea. 'While it is true that the moon-god has banished the evil spirit,' he mused, 'may not another come to take its place once the god has departed this land?'

After the celebrations the priests of Khonsu together with the physician Tehuti-em-heb made ready to depart, but when they came to take their leave of the King he was sorrowful and informed them that their immediate departure was impossible due to the heavy falls of snow in the mountain passes. Thus did Khonsu and his attendants remain in Bakhtan.

Time passed and again the priests and physician bade the King farewell, but this time the King told them that a tribe of fierce bandits now made the mountain ways impassable.

After this further delay, again the priests insisted that they must leave only to be told that an army of the Hatti were on the march to make war on Egypt so travel now would be extremely dangerous. Thus did the King of Bakhtan keep the image of Khonsu the Contriver within the boundaries of his realm. Since the god's arrival the land had been fruitful, the demons of plague had not troubled its people and all were happy and prosperous.

For three years the King of Bakhtan used various tales and stratagems to benefit from the power of the god until one night with the light of the moon streaming through his window he awoke in a cold sweat for he had had a vivid dream. Within his vision he had seen the moon-god's image rise from its small shrine in the form of a man to stare him straight in the eyes. The King feared that the anger of the god would strike him blind at the very least, but then Khonsu had taken on his hawk shape, each feather being made of the finest gold. Rising into the air the god circled Bakhtan three times saying, 'Free me O King, or all the good that has come of my presence will be replaced by a curse more terrible than that which you have previously known.' With this utterance the falcon flew off in the direction of Egypt.

Before the rise of the sun the King summoned the Egyptians and bade them make ready their departure from his land. He confessed his guilt to the priests and begged them to intercede with their god on behalf of his people. Then he ordered his servants to bring forth many presents for the shrine of Khonsu at Thebes for Bakhtan, under the patronage of that god, was no longer as poor as it once had been.

That day the whole population of the country came out to watch as the procession of Egyptians bore the image of Khonsu from their country. The long journey to the south was without incident for the power of the moon-god was with them and sooner than any mortal had thought possible they arrived at Thebes of the Hundred Gates to be greeted by the Pharaoh and his beautiful queen. Joining the procession, Ramesses and Neferure were borne aloft along with the statue of Khonsu the Contriver as they made their way to the temple of Karnak to give thanks for the deliverance of the Queen's sister.

Within the precincts of the temple the small statue of Khonsu was placed before the larger idol of the god of whom it was but a part. Magically, it returned the power which had been lent to it, as the many presents from Bakhtan were deposited in the sight of the great god, keeping nothing for itself. Then the small image of Khonsu the Contriver, now also named Khonsu Expeller of Demons was taken from that place and returned to its own more humble shrine, reaching its home on the nineteenth day of the second month of winter in the thirty-third year of the reign of Ramesses the Great, Meryamun, Usermaatre, Setepenra, Pharaoh of Upper and Lower Egypt and Lord of All the Lands, Beloved of Amun-Ra, fashioned by the gods, the holder of justice and chosen of the sun.

KHAEMWASET AND THE MUMMIES

RAMESSES THE GREAT, Pharaoh of Upper and Lower Egypt, Lord of All the Lands had married, during the course of his long reign, many wives, and had a harem of many concubines. But, far surpassing his queens in number, the children he fathered totalled no less than one hundred and ninety-eight, these being ninety-two sons and one hundred and six daughters.

Prince Khaemwaset was the child of the Great Royal Wife Istnofret and the eleventh son of the mighty King, and was undoubtedly the most perceptive and intelligent of the Pharaoh's extensive offspring.

Recognizing the boy's gift for learning, the Pharaoh appointed him to the exalted position of High Priest of Ptah at Memphis, the temple enclosures of that wise, craftsman god being the best place for the nurturing of a developing intellect. Indeed, as Khaemwaset grew so did his learning and with it his curiosity, mingled, it must be admitted, with some considerable arrogance. Yet the prince was possessed of a good heart and was noted for his many acts of kindness even if his insatiable desire for knowledge did occasionally lead him astray.

As was the course of things Ramesses eventually chose a wife for his son and Khaemwaset was married to a girl of good breeding and aristocratic birth. With her he was content for she provided a happy and harmonious home to complement his endless search for wisdom in the enclosures of the temple.

The years passed swiftly and children were born to the loving couple. These infants won favour both in the eyes of their father and in those of their awesome grandfather Ramesses the King.

Khaemwaset was now a grown man whose knowledge of the world, of the divinities, of nature and the arts of magic won him respect and admiration throughout the kingdoms of his father. It was, however, the occult arts that engaged most of the prince's attention for throughout his life he had wished to fathom the mysteries of

the universe and to attain the omniscient powers of a god.

Though Khaemwaset occasionally accompanied his father to new wars of conquest, the priest-prince spent most of his time in the libraries of his patron god Ptah. It was between the groaning shelves and rotting papyrus scrolls that Khaemwaset discovered a clue to the magical power that he had long sought. In a scroll so ancient that the hieroglyphs were cracked and faded, the prince read of a magician named Neferkaptah who had possessed a spell-book of such potent power that all the mysteries of the universe obeyed his will.

'Neferkaptah was a prince, the younger son of a long-forgotten pharaoh …' read Khaemwaset, beginning to feel a sense of kinship, '… and in the course of time he was married according to custom to a lady by the name of Ahwere who soon grew large with child. The child was named Mer-ib and found such favour in the eyes of his grandfather the pharaoh that he was spoken of as a future ruler of the Two Lands. Prince Neferkaptah was not thought suitable for this exalted role because he lacked worldly ambition and loved nothing better than to delve into the archives of the temples to discover hidden and forgotten knowledge.' Khaemwaset paused for a moment for the tale so far read like his own life.

'One day Neferkaptah went to the temple of ibis-headed Thoth to pray,' continued the story. 'But once there his eye was captured by the beauty and mystery of the thousands of paintings and carvings which adorned the holy place. Soon he was reading them avidly, for being a scholar of the old ways such things were within his power. Thus engrossed Neferkaptah forgot his duty and did not pray or make the customary libations to the god, but stood for hours patiently deciphering the meaning of obscure hieroglyphs in the hope of adding to his already considerable store of knowledge. As the sky-boat of Ra was setting in the west, Neferkaptah became aware of a chuckling behind him. Turning, he spied a figure standing in the lengthening shadows. "Why do you laugh at me?" asked the scholar-prince. The figure moved forward revealing itself to be a very old, yet vigorous-looking, man carrying the staff of a magician.

'"I laugh at your pathetic attempts to seek wisdom from these worthless writings," replied the stranger.

'Angry now, Neferkaptah spat back, "Then tell me where true wisdom lies if you are so clever."

"'That I will," said the old man calmly, "for I can tell you the location of the fabled Book of Thoth, the true repository of all magic, godly power and dark secrets which under-pin the universe."

'Shocked, Neferkaptah fought for words, "That is but an old lie and, in any case, even if such a book did exist it has not been seen since the time of King Chephren long in the past."

"'The Book exists," insisted the sage, "for the great god Thoth wrote it with his own hand, and in it is all the magic in the dominion of Ra. On the first page are spells to enchant the sky, the earth, the lands of the dead, the mountains and the Great

Green Sea. You will understand and speak the language of the birds of the air and the serpents who crawl upon the ground and are the wisest of beasts. You will see into the depths of the waters and understand the secrets of the deeps."

'Speechless, Neferkaptah could only gape.

'"The second page is more terrible," continued the stranger. "On it are written spells which can restore a long-dead soul to his mortal body. It contains charms which can enchant the dead and cause them to reveal the location of treasures and to prophesy that which is to come. Also, you will know the true nature of the sun, moon and stars, and be able to see the deathless gods in their immortal glory."

'His courage rising now, Neferkaptah declared, "Then by the life of my father the Pharaoh I will possess this book. Tell me old one, what will you take for the knowledge which you possess?"

'"As you say, I am old," said the sage nodding. "I ask nothing more than that you provide for my funeral for my earthly days will now be few. See that I am entombed as befits a rich man even though my means are paltry. Ensure that there are priests and mourning women, that the correct offerings are made and that plentiful incense is burned. One hundred pieces of silver should be sufficient to satisfy the needs of my Ka in the afterlife."

'Without delay, Neferkaptah sent a messenger to his house for the requisite funds and, as soon as these had been delivered into the old man's hands, he brought his wrinkled, dry mouth close to the prince's ear. "The Book of Thoth lies in the midst of the Nile close to Koptos. In the middle of the sacred river is a sarcophagus made of iron, within it is a chest made of bronze. In the bronze chest there is a box made of kete-wood, and within that is a box wrought of ivory and ebony. Locked within these is a box of silver, within which is a box of gold and at its heart is the Book of Thoth. But beware, for all about these strong containers are serpents, scorpions and many other noxious crawling things which will wish to do you harm. The greatest peril, though, is a huge river snake which has been so enchanted that it cannot be killed by the hand of man." So saying, the old man straightened somewhat as if a terrible burden had been lifted from his shoulders and, bidding the scholar-prince farewell, he shuffled away into the shadows.

'Neferkaptah was in no mood for warnings of dire consequences. His heart was filled with the desire to possess this marvellous book so he hastened to his home and roused his sleeping wife Ahwere to tell her all that had befallen.

'However, Ahwere was troubled by her husband's revelation and begged him not to embark on such a dangerous quest. Yet heedless of her plea, Neferkaptah went to his father the King begging him for a royal barge to bear him and his family southwards. The Pharaoh was saddened by this sudden desire of his son and counselled him to remain at court for a while until further investigations could be made. "Such power is not without its price my son, and through the misuse of the magic you, your wife Ahwere and your child Mer-ib may be struck down by the wrath of the deathless gods." But Neferkaptah would heed no words of caution, so sadly the King commanded that all be done as his son wished.

'Soon Neferkaptah, Ahwere and Mer-ib were speeding southwards aboard the royal barge. Swift though the voyage was, it was not swift enough to suit the prince who grew ever more eager to possess the Book of Thoth.

'On their arrival at Koptos, Neferkaptah was dismayed to find that the priestesses of Isis had come to greet them, and convey them to their temple to honour the powerful goddess. With ill-concealed impatience, Neferkaptah complied with their wishes and sacrificed an ox and a goose to the mistress of magic and her son Horus.

'Neferkaptah's dismay turned to frustrated anguish when he discovered that a celebration planned to last for four days had been arranged to mark the visit of the Pharaoh's son to Koptos. Ahwere, for her part, was secretly glad and hoped that the festivities of the next few days would distract her husband from the sinister magic that lay at the bottom of the Nile.

'At first Neferkaptah smiled amiably at his hosts and praised the music and the singing, but as time went on and entertainment followed entertainment, becoming ever more extravagant and drunken, the prince's face began to show his displeasure.

'Be that as it may be, it was not until the dawning of his fifth day in Koptos that Neferkaptah called on the chief priest of Isis to aid him in his endeavour. Together, the two called on sorcerous arts to construct a little box much like the cabin of a boat. They carved miniature men from wood and wove tiny ship's tackle from twine. These they carefully placed in the cabin. Then, leaving the priest to his holy work, the prince took his precious box down to the river's edge. He then breathed upon the little cabin and uttered a powerful spell in the name of Isis which brought the tiny men to life. At once they began to fill the royal barge with sand and when this was accomplished Neferkaptah boarded and left Koptos and his sad wife Ahwere behind him.

'The little wooden men returned to the tiny cabin and the prince said, "Workmen, work-men, work for me," as he dropped the box, workmen, tackle and all into the river. Down into the depths they sank until at length they came to rest on the mud at the bottom of the Nile. For three days and three nights the little men toiled beneath the waters. They dug and

delved into the mud and, when they had searched in one place for long enough, they would move on to another; as they moved, far above the royal barge moved also, always keeping pace with the tiny labourers. Then they moved no more and Neferkaptah, standing at the prow of the barge, knew that they had found the iron sarcophagus. Their purpose fulfilled, the workmen had become carved wood once more.

'Now the sorcerer-prince tipped the sand he had brought into the sacred Nile all the while muttering spells and flattering Hapi the river-god. With a roaring sound the waters parted as a great whirlpool appeared leading downwards to the very riverbed – and there lay the rusting, ancient sarcophagus. On all sides of this metal coffin were snakes and scorpions and many other venomous things that Neferkaptah could not name, but more terrifying than all of these was the huge serpent which lay coiled about the iron box.

'All at once the force of the whirlpool seized the barge and propelled it down to the bed of the river. Neferkaptah was unafraid for his magical arts protected him.

'When the boat reached the muddy floor the scorpions and crawling things advanced to work their fatal mischief upon this intruder but Neferkaptah remained calm and spoke a powerful spell which rendered the creeping terrors immobile. Alighting then, Neferkaptah drew his sword as he walked across the soft mud towards the sarcophagus. The great serpent, which had been charged by the very gods to guard the precious coffin, reared up from the ooze. With no hesitation, the sorcerer-prince lunged forward and severed its repulsive head from its body with one blow but, instead of expiring, the head and body were drawn together once more. It was only Neferkaptah's swift reflexes that saved him from immediate death as the monster struck, its wicked fangs dripping venom. Again, the prince attacked, and again did the serpent's head fly from its body only to reunite with dazzling speed. Neferkaptah escaped the next assault but knew that he could not do so a third time. When he again severed the creature's head he took a handful of sand and thrust it into the monster's neck-stump thus preventing the reunion of the deathless serpent which lay impotently thrashing on the slimy ground.

'This enemy now dealt with, Neferkaptah took hold of the sarcophagus and, with a mighty effort, forced open the iron lid. Within, as the old man had prophesied, was a chest of bronze which he also opened. Breathless now, he forced open box after box until the golden casket lay beneath his gaze. With trembling fingers, he lifted the lid to find himself bathed in an unnatural radiance for within lay the fabled Book of Thoth itself. Lifting the ancient scroll Neferkaptah stumbled back to the barge which lifted itself from the river's bed as the whirlpool reversed its course allowing the sacred Nile to return to its normal flow.

'Once more on the water's surface, the enraptured Neferkaptah opened the scroll and read. At once he learned the awesome power to enchant the sky, the earth, the lands of the dead, the mountains and the Great Green Sea. He now knew how to understand and speak the language of the birds of the air and that of the serpents which crawl upon the ground. He could gaze into the depths of the waters and understand the secrets of the deeps.

'Still trembling, Neferkaptah then turned the papyrus around and read the second page. Immediately he knew how to restore a long-dead soul to his mortal body. He learned how to enchant the dead and cause them to reveal the location of hidden treasures and to prophesy that which is to come. In addition the true nature of the sun, the moon and the stars were revealed to him. Tears streaming from his eyes, Neferkaptah looked up into the sky and saw the deathless gods in their immortal glory sailing in the boat of the sun.

'Only after all these wonders did Neferkaptah cry out, "Workmen, workmen, work for me and return me to my wife at Koptos." Far beneath him on the river's floor the little carved men came alive again. They marched in unison across the mud in the direction of Koptos and, as they did so, the barge moved across the surface keeping pace with them.

'Ahwere had spent a long time on the shore of the Nile awaiting her husband's return so when she saw the barge she was overjoyed and called for her son to attend her and to greet his father properly. But Neferkaptah had no time for such ceremony and leapt from the deck before the barge had berthed and, taking them both in his arms, laughed and laughed with the joy of his accomplishment. When his exhilaration had faded he put the Book of Thoth into Ahwere's hands and bade her read it. As she did so, the power of the gods surged through her body and she too shared her husband's new-found supernatural qualities.

'The boy, Mer-ib, was the next to partake of the divine glory so now all three felt themselves to be more than merely human. Neferkaptah then carefully inscribed a copy of the precious book on a new piece of papyrus. When his ink was dry he scraped off his carefully formed hieroglyphs and poured the inky powder into a cup of beer. This he drank thus ensuring that the powers he had gained would never be able to leave him for they now flowed within every particle of his body.

'Unknown to these fated three, the great god Thoth had learned of the theft of his book and raged like a panther at its loss. Hastening to the mighty sun-god Ra he made an impassioned plea for vengeance. At this, Ra gazed down from the sky-boat to see that Neferkaptah, his wife and son were sailing homeward upon the royal barge. He drew the boy Mer-ib into the water and stifled his new-found magic; thus did he drown in the sacred waters of the Nile and Thoth was glad.

'Ahwere and Neferkaptah wept piteously at the sight of their poor son's little dead body and the course of the barge was changed to return to Koptos to have him embalmed as was the custom. As they returned the awful force of Ra's will went forth again, smothering the powers of Ahwere, who was flung out of the boat into the churning waters. She, too, perished there, eventually to be netted and pulled on to the barge's deck by her husband who was now beside himself with grief. But the great god Thoth was not satisfied with the deaths of mother and son and sent a madness to afflict Neferkaptah who called upon the magic within him to summon the soul of his son back for a brief time to comfort his aching heart. The corpse of the boy twitched and rose but did not speak as he had done in his short earthly life.

'"O Father," he began, "we are victims of the vengeance of the gods, for you have stolen that which was forbidden even to the sages of old." So saying, the boy lay down and was a corpse once more. Despair gripped every part of the prince's being so he too threw himself into the waters. He spoke no spell to ensure his safety nor did he cast any charm about him. Thus did Neferkaptah, Prince of Egypt, die.

'The power of Thoth then raised Neferkaptah's body from the river, placing it on the deck of the barge next to his son and wife and thus were they found by the Pharaoh of the Two Lands as he journeyed southwards to discover their fate.

'Putting on mourning garb, the Pharaoh commanded that the three be entombed together with all their goods at Saqqara and it is there in the very tomb that the King

had hewn for his son that the mighty Book of Thoth now lies hidden from the eyes of mortal men. Thus is the will of the great god Thoth, master of learning, satisfied. All this was set down as a warning by the will of the Pharaoh.'

When he had finished reading this ancient tale, Khaemwaset was feverish with excitement. Ignoring the warnings within the story he thereupon resolved to find the tomb of Neferkaptah, to breach its sealed portals and to make the book of spells his own. However, it was to be many more months before the prince found the lost tomb which lay beneath the desert sand at Saqqara near to the famous stepped pyramid of the long-dead Pharaoh Djoser.

First, Khaemwaset sent to his younger half-brother Anhureru to enlist his aid in his quest. Bidding his wife and children farewell, the priest-prince and his brother departed secretly from Memphis and, crossing the sacred Nile, proceeded into the desert. Once they had arrived at

Saqqara, the two princes used the great stepped pyramid as a marker. Together with the configurations of certain stars it led them to the very site of the hidden tomb.

For three nights they laboured, resting during the heat of the day, until the massive portal which sealed the tomb was cleared of sand. They then set to work breaking the stone barrier sufficiently to allow them into the shrouded interior itself.

Crawling through the narrow gap that they had created, Khaemwaset and Anhureru entered the mortuary passageway that led to the inner chambers of the tomb. Carefully they moved past the veiled figure of the crouching jackal-god Anubis, the tomb's guardian, and opened the creaking door that led to the sarcophagi within. As they did so the pair were amazed to see that the inner chamber was flooded with light which radiated from the precious scroll of magic which lay on a dais between the two larger of the three sarcophagi within the gorgeously decorated sanctum. Khaemwaset was delighted to see that the object of their search was a talisman of such power but, as he reached forth his hand to take it, the heavy lids of the granite coffins shifted and rose as the mummies of Neferkaptah, his wife Ahwere and the small Mer-ib shook off the pall of death.

Anhureru shook with terror and, had his legs obeyed his will, would have fled from the dreadful sight, but Khaemwaset stood his ground and did not reveal the fear that was turning his entrails to water.

Spitting dust from his long dry mouth the bandaged corpse of Neferkaptah spoke, the echoes of the centuries resonating in his voice. 'Rash intruders, who are you that dares to disturb the eternal rest of Neferkaptah and his kin?'

Suppressing the shaking of his voice Khaemwaset replied, 'I am the son of Ramesses the Pharaoh and thus the blood of gods runs in my veins. Also I am a great magician favoured by the wise god Ptah so take care O relic for I can defend myself with powerful spells.' The three mummies began to sigh softly as dust cascaded from their cerements. Khaemwaset realized that they were laughing at him.

'You have come to this place of death for one purpose and that is to seize the accursed scroll of dark secrets,' coughed the corpse of Neferkaptah, 'for you are an impudent youth who has lured your weak-minded companion into following a path that is not only unwise, but fatal. Your own unwisdom does not do justice to the patronage of Ptah.' All the while the two mummies of Ahwere and Mer-ib never ceased their eerie hissing laughter. 'Do you consider yourself wise enough to possess this sacred scroll which is none other than the fabled Book of Thoth?' enquired the rasping Neferkaptah.

'My wisdom was sufficient to discover the existence of the scroll,' replied Khaemwaset, his poise returning. 'My knowledge was sufficient to discover this tomb and my skill was sufficient to gain access to this burial chamber where you eke out a miserable half-life beneath the earth. Thus am I a fitting keeper for the magic of the scroll which contains the knowledge of the wisest god of them all.'

'I gave my earthly life for the magic of the scroll,' croaked the mummy. 'Its power destroyed my mortal being, and those of my wife and child. Do you think that we would part with it so easily?'

'Your tale is familiar to me and very sad,' said Khaemwaset, 'but my purpose is clear and I will possess the scroll.'

'Then let us act as civilized men.' The voice of Neferkaptah rattled as he adopted a more reasonable tone. 'Let us wager over a game of senet, to the winner the magic of the scroll.'

To this suggestion Khaemwaset readily agreed for there were few in the upper world who could beat him at the senet board. The sorry cadavers of Neferkaptah's wife and child gathered the board and pieces with many a creak and groan from their rotting joints, setting the game between them. Thus was semblance given of a match between life and death.

Each took a turn in throwing the sticks. Khaemwaset threw jackals, while Neferkaptah's mummy scored fingers. So, Neferkaptah made the first move. As the game progressed it became obvious that the long-dead Neferkaptah was a skilled player and Khaemwaset began to doubt the wisdom of agreeing to this game.

'The Book of Thoth is a most valuable item is it not?' asked Khaemwaset idly.

'Indeed it is, foolish prince,' replied the mummy.

'Then to decide the fate of such a marvellous volume upon one game of senet, is almost blasphemous,' stated the prince.

'It would appear to be so,' croaked Neferkaptah.

'Then let us continue to play until one of us admits defeat, the better to mark this occasion,' suggested Khaemwaset.

'As you will,' agreed the corpse, who by now had won the first game.

As the last piece was placed on the board Neferkaptah declared himself to be the winner. Suddenly, he lifted the board and struck Khaemwaset a great blow on the head. Though stunned Khaemwaset then felt a strange heaviness about his feet. Looking down, he saw to his horror that both his feet had sunk into the floor of the tomb up to his ankle bones and he was unable to move them. All the while the rotting spectres of Mer-ib and Ahwere arranged the senet board for the next game.

The game proceeded as before with Neferkaptah skilfully capturing and isolating the pieces of Khaemwaset. Again did the crumbling Neferkaptah achieve victory and again did he strike Khaemwaset on the head. This time, though, Khaemwaset sank up to the very joints of his knees.

As the board was being arranged for the third game, Khaemwaset called for his brother Anhureru who had, for all this time, stood frozen in terror at the doorway. 'Brother, leave this place and run to our father to tell him of my predicament and to implore his help.' Anhureru did not pause to reply but fled the tomb, scrambling upwards through the passageways until he stood in the sun once more. Hardly pausing to catch his breath, he ran to his mule and made all haste to the city of Memphis where Ramesses the Great was holding court.

The young Prince Anhureru did not stand on ceremony but roughly pushed past the royal attendants until he stood in the presence of his father the King. He quickly explained his rudeness and told of the danger in which Khaemwaset found himself. At this dire news Ramesses removed from about his neck an amulet in the form of the scarab Khepera, the dawning sun. Then, with a speed that outdid his flight, Anhureru returned to the Saqqara tomb. Descending into the gloom, Anhureru first heard the soft hissing laughter of the mummies as they again rejoiced at yet another victory at the gaming board. Emerging into the eerily lit burial chamber, Anhureru was horrified to see that his brother had now sunk into the ground so far that only his head and his right arm were still visible.

Following the instructions of Ramesses, Anhureru placed the scarab amulet on his imperilled brother's head. At once, the ground threw him up until he towered above the senet board which had been his undoing. At this the three mummies ceased their ghastly cackling and reached for him, but Khaemwaset was too swift for their ancient, clumsy fingers. Leaping past them he seized the magical scroll and thrust it beneath his robe, extinguishing the unnatural light and plunging the tomb into stygian blackness. Anhureru called out and, by following the sound of his fleeing brother's voice, Khaemwaset escaped from the chamber. Yet as the two bedraggled princes emerged into sunlight the thin voice of Neferkaptah followed them, 'Foolish mortals, the book which you hold will bring nought but grief and misery to you and all your kin. I prophesy that you will bring it into the tomb of your own free will.'

Laughing with relief, the two princes took no heed of the mummy's bitter words and set out for Memphis and the court of their father. But though Khaemwaset gave every sign of good humour, his heart was chilled with nameless dread.

At the court of Memphis the two princes, both shrouded in the dust of the tomb and the desert, were looking less than princely as they entered their father's presence. Ramesses was stern and demanded that Khaemwaset give an account of himself. When he was done, the Pharaoh's demeanour was even more grave. 'Have you yet opened the scroll my son?' he enquired.

'No, Father, for as you can plainly see I have not so much as broken the seal that was set upon it so many years ago,' replied Khaemwaset.

'Then perhaps no lasting damage has been done,' said the Pharaoh. 'My advice to you is to return this accursed book to the tomb from whence it came and beg forgiveness of the mummified guardians and of the great god Thoth himself. However, to re-enter the tomb safely you must carry a forked stick to repel the evil spells sent against you and you must bear a lighted brazier above your head. This is my advice which I, your father and King, urge you to follow.'

Khaemwaset was silent for a while as he considered the words of Ramesses for he had no wish to lose the Book of Thoth which he had gained by so many trials and in peril of his life. 'By your Majesty's leave I will go to the temple of Ptah and meditate upon your counsel.' Khaemwaset then bowed low and departed from the royal court. Arriving at the temple, Khaemwaset hastened to his rooms where he hid the still unopened scroll of Thoth in a heavy chest for the terrible experience of the tomb and the harsh words of his father had frightened him.

Some days later Khaemwaset was walking in the huge courtyard of the temple of Ptah when he saw a beautiful woman strolling with her attendants in the shade of the colonnades. Her skin was pale, her hair lustrous and dark, her body lithe and supple while her great dark golden-green eyes held all the promise of every pleasure in the world. About her wrists were bracelets of the finest gold, while her necklace and head-dress were of silver worked with the dazzling azure of lapis lazuli. All thoughts of his wife and children flew from his mind as Khaemwaset was over-whelmed with love for this wondrous being. He forgot his position as the son of the Pharaoh and his high post as the chief priest of Ptah. He also forgot all about the scroll of terrible power that lay within his rooms, for all the lust which he had felt for the Book of Thoth was as nothing compared to his desire for this woman. His dignity was stripped from him and he would gladly have walked barefoot through the burning sands of the desert to win one smile from her alluring lips. Finding him-self unable to approach the beautiful vision directly, Khaemwaset ordered a page to find out all he could about her. The page went up to one of the lady's serving women and gained the information that his master so desperately wanted. Returning to Khaemwaset, the page told him that the lady's name was Tabibu, a daughter of the priest of the cat-goddess Bast, whose shrine was in the town of Ankhtawy. 'She has come to Memphis,' continued the boy, 'to worship at the altar of Ptah and would welcome the presence of the chief priest of that god at her devotions.'

Unable to believe his luck, Khaemwaset tried to gather his courage to make himself known to the lady while sending his page on another errand to the serving woman. 'My master, Khaemwaset, the chief priest of Ptah wishes to know if your mistress would consent to spend an hour alone with him. If her answer is yes then he will give her a present of ten gold pieces to prove his devotion. If the lady fears scandal or accusations I am bidden to say that the chief priest will settle all to her satisfaction for all will be arranged with the utmost discretion.'

Appalled by this suggestion, the woman struck the boy across the head while berating him and his importunate master. At the sound of the woman's raised voice Tabibu demanded to know what the noise was about. Barely holding back his tears the boy again repeated his master's question. Tabibu paused for thought before replying, 'Go to Khaemwaset and tell him that I am a lady of high rank, and no woman of the streets. Tell him that if he wishes to spend time with me he must come to my house in the city of Bubastis where the feline race is sacred and men shave their eyebrows as a sign of mourning when a cat dies. In that place there will be discretion enough and I will be at his disposal for in Bubastis, city of love, no one will say that I have acted like a common harlot.' With these words, she and her attendants departed the temple of Ptah.

When the message was repeated to Khaemwaset he was rapturous with joy. He at once sought out the company of his half-brother Anhureru to tell him the news. But, far from being pleased, Anhureru reminded Khaemwaset of his duties as High Priest of Ptah, the son of the Pharaoh and as a married man and father. These words of good sense swayed Khaemwaset not at all, and he left his kinsman with anger in his heart. With more resolve than ever, Khaemwaset ordered that his boat be put in order and that his crewmen prepare for a voyage to the delta and the city of Bubastis.

Arriving at the city, Prince Khaemwaset soon found the house of Tabibu. It was tall and fine, with a terrace before the main door and a fertile garden set to the north. It was into this shady grove that he was shown while his presence was announced to the lady. Soon, the sultry Tabibu came through the trees. Taking Khaemwaset warmly by the hand she spoke softly.

'Is it your will that we should go at once to my bedchamber O son of Pharaoh?' she purred. Without waiting for a reply she led the bemused prince through the house to a splendid room decorated in turquoise, gold and lapis lazuli. She poured wine into a golden cup and brought it to the prince's lips. 'Will you eat, Lord of Memphis?' she enquired. Before Khaemwaset could reply the finest viands were brought by slaves who set a table between the pair. 'Would you have music, wise priest?' Tabibu sighed. Yet again before Khaemwaset could respond, musicians

entered the fine room and began to play. After some time Khaemwaset's passion was as red and fierce as his impatience.

'Tabibu, is it for wine, food and music that I have come here? Let us now do that which I have come here to do.' Tabibu regarded him over the rim of her cup, her eyes as wise as a sacred cat.

'Did I not tell you that I am no common woman? If you would have me then you must draw up a deed of maintenance on my behalf so that I will be recognized as your mistress.'

At this Khaemwaset cried out, 'Then send for a scribe to write down the details for I am so in love with you that I swear that all I own will be yours.' The scribe came swiftly and set down details of his wealth, his properties and his titles, all of which were now to be transferred to the ownership of Tabibu of Bubastis.

'Now, let us continue,' said Khaemwaset, 'for all you have asked of me has been done and I now long to engage in love-play with you.'

'Should you not first greet your half-brother and your young children who have come to this house to find you?' enquired the temptress, feigning innocence as she put on a robe of sheer cloth through which every curve of her body was so visible that Khaemwaset's desire was even more impassioned than before.

'No,' he replied. 'Let them wait and let us do that which I have come here to do.' At that moment, Anhureru and the children were ushered into the room.

'If you desire me, remember that I am no common woman, otherwise you must return to your own house,' said Tabibu. 'Let your brother and children also sign the document the scribe has prepared so there will be no difficulties between them and the children I shall bear you.' So, Khaemwaset commanded his children to witness the document and that Anhureru also give his consent.

Weeping, Anhureru and the children huddled in a corner of the room unable to believe that Khaemwaset could betray them so thoroughly. 'Let us now make love,' demanded Khaemwaset but Tabibu's wiles were not yet exhausted.

'Your children are still a danger to me, as is your half-brother. Have them killed at once so that they may not complain to the Pharaoh.'

Khaemwaset was horrified but his lust was all-consuming. 'Let this terrible thing be done then, since you find it necessary.' At once armed guards entered and hacked Anhureru and the children to pieces before his eyes. The pathetic, bleeding remains were bundled up and thrown out of the window to be licked by the cats below.

'Now truly I have done all you have asked,' moaned Khaemwaset. 'Let us now do that which I have come here to do.'

At this Tabibu rose and, taking him by the hand brought him to a room with a bed made of ivory and ebony. Tabibu let her robe slip from her shoulders and lay down naked beneath Khaemwaset's lustful gaze. He reached out to her but, as his hand touched her breast, Tabibu opened her lovely mouth and let out a terrible scream. Immediately a veil lifted from Khaemwaset's eyes; the bedchamber, the ebony and ivory bed and Tabibu herself became insubstantial and illusory and the prince found himself naked and sweating, covered in the dust of the desert. Shaking with fear and unspent passion Khaemwaset saw that near to his right hand was the very Book of Thoth which he had thought safely locked away in his rooms at the temple.

A cloud of dust then rose from the horizon as the chariot of Ramesses the Pharaoh, attended by many guards and runners, came into view. Spying his dishevelled son grovelling in the dirt, the King called out, 'Khaemwaset, how is it that I find you in this filthy condition?'

'Oh father,' groaned Khaemwaset, 'it is all the fault of the long-dead Neferkaptah who has enchanted me and stripped me of my dignity. It is his magic that has caused me to give away all my property and, worse even than this, to have my own brother and my children slain.' Khaemwaset then told his father of all that had transpired with Tabibu of Bubastis.

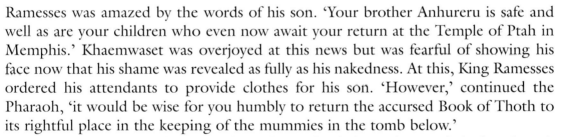

Ramesses was amazed by the words of his son. 'Your brother Anhureru is safe and well as are your children who even now await your return at the Temple of Ptah in Memphis.' Khaemwaset was overjoyed at this news but was fearful of showing his face now that his shame was revealed as fully as his nakedness. At this, King Ramesses ordered his attendants to provide clothes for his son. 'However,' continued the Pharaoh, 'it would be wise for you humbly to return the accursed Book of Thoth to its rightful place in the keeping of the mummies in the tomb below.'

Khaemwaset tucked the magical scroll into his belt, took up a forked stick and, holding a lighted brazier above his head, descended into the gloom of the sepulchre. He entered the burial chamber to find no evidence that the mummies of Neferkaptah, Ahwere or Mer-ib had ever moved, for all was in place and all the grave goods seemed undisturbed. Even so, Khaemwaset spoke aloud a warm greeting to his long-dead hosts and reverently replaced the awesome Book of Thoth on its plinth between the two largest sarcophagi. Again did Khaemwaset speak humbly to the dead as he bade them farewell.

As he walked back towards his father's chariot a sandstorm suddenly blew up, covering the entrance to the tomb for ever. However, it seemed to Khaemwaset that the wind itself spoke to him and him alone in the sighing voice of Neferkaptah, 'Count yourself fortunate young prince that no further harm ensued from your theft of a book that is the property of the gods themselves.' With this in mind, a wiser Khaemwaset and the royal entourage set off for the city of Memphis once more.

SE-OSIRIS

IN THE FULLNESS OF TIME PRINCE Khaemwaset was declared heir to the throne of his father Ramesses the Great for it was considered that his knowledge of times past, his prowess in battle and his mastery of the arts of magic would make him an ideal pharaoh when the mighty King's days were past.

But all was not happy at the court, for the children of Khaemwaset and his beloved wife Mahitouaskhit had died one by one, and now they had no living children at all. Thus the Princess Mahitouaskhit went to Memphis, to the temple of Imhotep, son of the great god Ptah the Cunning, to pray that she be made fruitful again.

In the depths of her sleep the princess was granted a dream in which she was directed to certain herbs and leaves which grew on the banks of the sacred Nile. From these she was to prepare a potion which when drunk would fulfil her desire for a son. On awakening, Mahitouaskhit immediately gathered the plants and made the elixir, and then took ship down the Nile to return to her husband at Thebes.

It was soon revealed that the princess was with child, and Khaemwaset used his magical arts to prepare amulets and spells to protect Mahitouaskhit and her unborn son from all manner of harm. When this was done Khaemwaset lay down to sleep, and while he slept he dreamt that he heard a voice which said: 'Khaemwaset, your wife Mahitouaskhit will give birth to a son who is to be named Se-Osiris. Through him many wonders will be accomplished throughout the Two Lands.' When the prince awoke he remembered the message and rejoiced.

When the boy was born, Khaemwaset

named him in accordance with the instruction in his dream. The child grew rapidly, soon outstripping all infants of his age. He learned to speak very quickly and, by the age of five years, the boy Se-Osiris could read the most complex hieroglyphs and argue the most obscure points of philosophy with the priests at the temple.

So proud was the loving father Khaemwaset that he brought him to court and challenged the cleverest magicians of the King to better the arts of his wonder-working son. Each sorcerer gave a demonstration of power only to find that this young boy could far surpass their finest efforts: the creation of a flower would be answered by a rain of petals from the air; the charming of a serpent would be made as nought next to the sight of the small boy Se-Osiris riding upon the back of a crocodile.

The Pharaoh Ramesses was captivated by his new grandson, and his pride equalled that of Khaemwaset. He lavished presents upon the boy and ensured that the world knew that Se-Osiris was high in royal favour.

One day Khaemwaset stood with his son on the terrace of the palace when they heard the loud laments of the lavish funeral procession of a nobleman. Shortly after this, the boy drew his father's attention to another sad scene. This time it was the body of a poor peasant wrapped in a simple straw mat and flung over the shoulder of a burly embalmer with none to mourn his passing.

'By all the gods,' remarked Khaemwaset, 'may it be that I come to the Land of the Dead in the manner of the nobleman, honoured and lamented, and not as this poor peasant who is already forgotten.'

'Father, it is the fate of the poor man that I wish for you, not the nobleman,' Se-Osiris replied. Khaemwaset felt wounded by his son, who looked gravely at his father and replied, 'I will show you the fates of these two, the nobleman so greatly mourned and the unlamented peasant.'

Then Se-Osiris spoke a powerful spell and suddenly they both stood in an unknown place far to the west of the mountains of Memphis. Here they saw seven great pillared halls filled with people of all ranks and fortunes. One by one they passed through these huge rooms observing all that went on among the dead who thronged them. They moved through three of these chambers without being accosted or hindered in any way but when they came to the fourth they saw that from the high ceiling hung all manner of foodstuffs. Here were roast duck, and oxen, fruit and a thousand different delicacies. The floor of the hall was in chaos for men and women were fighting fiercely and attempting to climb over each other to take hold of the food which was just a finger's breadth out of reach.

Khaemwaset and Se-Osiris were careful to dodge through the mêleé and thus came to the fifth hall, the doorway of which was surrounded by pathetic shades who had committed terrible crimes and could go no further. The door itself pivoted in the eye socket of one of these unfortunates who wailed and groaned as Khaemwaset and Se-Osiris opened it to pass through. Within the next hall, which was brightly lit, father and son were surrounded by spirits who had followed the just and true ways of the goddess Maat and had achieved tranquillity. In the sixth hall the gods of the after world sat in judgement, for these were the arbiters of Maat. The seventh hall was the most splendid of all for this was the throne room of the great Osiris himself. The god sat poised upon a golden throne, wearing the White Crown plumed with the feathers of Maat. A greenish cast infused his godly face and he bore the Crook and Flail of sovereignty in his gentle hands. To his left stood his elder son Anubis, the jackal-headed god of tombs, and on his right stood ibis-headed Thoth, god of wisdom and recorder of the court of the immortals. Before this divine trio stood the scales which weighed the virtues and vices of the souls of the dead. By its tilt, guilt or innocence were established as the very heart of the deceased was measured against the feather of Maat. Anubis pronounced the judgement which Thoth then transcribed. Those whose sins condemned them were destroyed utterly; those whose sins were of equal measure to their virtues entered the twilight world of the mummified hawk-god Seker; and those who were without fault took their place amongst the gods and the blessed dead.

Khaemwaset then noticed that near to the throne of Osiris was a man of high rank dressed in the finest of garments. Se-Osiris told him that this was none other than the unmourned peasant whose mat-bound body they had seen so rudely treated. 'This man's virtues so outweighed the feather of Maat that he will dwell among the gods for ever,' said Se-Osiris.

'But what of the nobleman?' asked Khaemwaset.

'His sins were great,' replied Se-Osiris gravely, 'so great indeed that he is now the man who screams as the mighty door pivots within his eye socket. This is the reason that I would wish that you endured the fate of the virtuous peasant rather than that of the greedy and selfish nobleman.'

Khaemwaset and his son left the Land of the Dead by the power of Se-Osiris, who dispelled the hungry ghosts with a word and took the blessings of the gods with them. Khaemwaset gave the revelations of his son much thought but did not speak of them to any man.

By the time that Se-Osiris was twelve years old there was no wise man, magician, priest or scribe who could equal him for learning or sorcerous prowess. It was at this time that the kings and princes of certain foreign lands challenged Ramesses to prove the superiority of Egypt. These kings well knew that they could not overcome the forces of the Pharaoh on the field of battle so they devised a series of cunning puzzles to befuddle the wits of the wisest men in the Two Lands. If they could not solve these mysteries then Egypt would be declared an inferior kingdom and unworthy of the primacy of the world.

Each king and prince formulated a riddle which was dispatched to Thebes of the Hundred Gates, the court of Ramesses. The Pharaoh, trusting in the wisdom of his newly declared heir, gave the task of solving them to Khaemwaset who answered each and every question with ease. So, one by one, the kings of Joppa, Kadesh, Aleppo, Meggido, Yehem and those of many other cities and countries declared that the wisdom of Egypt was indeed superior to their own and renewed their offerings of tribute to the mighty Ramesses.

But the King of Nubia, far to the south, was not satisfied and sent an emissary to Thebes of the Hundred Gates to confront the Pharaoh; and one day, an ancient, rascally looking Nubian was brought before Ramesses. The furtive visitor declared himself to be the ambassador of the King of Nubia, even though he was not arrayed as was customary for a person who held such a post. Neither did he bring gifts or present either the credentials or the good wishes of his sovereign. Instead, the old beggar handed Ramesses a sealed scroll saying, 'Here is a sealed letter from my king. If any man can read its contents without breaking the seal then will Nubia declare the supremacy of the Pharaoh of Egypt. However, if no one can accomplish this feat then Egypt will be shown to be an unworthy kingdom and its Pharaoh a fool.'

The great Ramesses frowned: 'Do not boast so readily O insolent one, for this is the home of wisdom and by the will of the gods your words will be regretted.'

The ragged ambassador left the royal presence as Ramesses summoned Khaemwaset, his heir. When this new puzzle was explained to him, Khaemwaset spoke. 'But who can read a letter unless it is opened and spread before him? Great King, my father give me ten days to solve this riddle.' His request was granted and Khaemwaset, his brow furrowed in deep thought, took the sealed letter and returned to his home. To mark the efforts of his son, Ramesses took an oath that he would fast until the day that Egypt could defeat the challenge of Nubia.

That night, Khaemwaset lay sleepless; in the morning, as the light of Ra filled the sky, Se-Osiris came to his father and asked what it was that so troubled his sleep.

'This is not a matter for a child,' replied Khaemwaset. But Se-Osiris persisted in his questioning until eventually the grave Khaemwaset told his son of the Nubian challenge and the mysterious sealed letter. As soon as his story was done Se-Osiris doubled up in mirth. He laughed so much that Khaemwaset grew angry.

'Do not be wrathful, father,' exclaimed the boy between bursts of laughter, 'for the matter of the sealed letter is but a little thing which I will accomplish for you without unrolling the scroll.'

Still raging, Khaemwaset scolded, 'How am I to know if you speak the truth boy?'

126

Calmly Se-Osiris replied, 'Go Father, fetch any book that you desire, place it before me, and I will read its contents fully without opening it.' At this, Khaemwaset rushed from the room to gather scrolls from his library. One by one he brought these to Se-Osiris who fulfilled his word and read each and every one simply by gazing at the rolled-up parchment before him.

On the tenth day, Khaemwaset and Se-Osiris came to the court of the Pharaoh. Ramesses had no doubts concerning the abilities of either his son or grandson and had prepared a feast to greet them. Later, they all made their way to the Hall of Audience, bowing low as Ramesses ascended to the Horus Throne. When all were

BES

THE MOST common lucky charm to be worn in Ancient Egypt was an image of the god Bes. This ugly, diminutive deity did not belong to the higher echelons of the great gods, but was immensely popular amongst the people. Probably African in origin, Bes may represent a pygmy wearing a lion mask and a plumed head-dress; he is also unusual in that he is shown full-faced rather than in profile, as was the convention in Egyptian art.

Known for his kindliness, Bes progressed from his role as protector of sheep and shepherds to presiding over revelry, dancing and inebriation (many of the Bes charms show the merry little god with a musical instrument). Marriages were also linked with the pygmy deity and he was associated with aiding women in childbirth; Bes is shown on the walls of the temple of Hatshepsut in Western Thebes in the scene depicting the birth of the great Queen.

As Bes was the guardian of children, he became the mortal enemy of serpents, scorpions or any creature that could do his charges harm.

in their appointed places, the doors were opened for the beggar-ambassador who, with insolent arrogance, demanded to be told the contents of the letter. At this the young Se-Osiris stood and placed a curse on the head of the rogue and on all of Nubia if he should dare to state that what was read was not true. The old ambassador agreed to this condition and again demanded to be told the scroll's contents.

Solemnly, Se-Osiris took the contentious scroll in his hands. Bowing his head, he closed his eyes and began to speak.

'Long ago, in the benevolent reign of the Pharaoh Manakphre-Siamon, when all was fruitful, the gods contented and the people happy, the King of Nubia took his ease in his pleasure pavilion close to a temple of Amun. While he rested there he heard three sorcerers talking amongst themselves. The first, speaking in a high-pitched voice, said that if Amun would preserve him he would put a dire spell on the land of Egypt so that a great darkness would shade the Nile and that men would not be able to see either the sun or the moon for three days and three nights. Then the second man spoke, "If Amun will preserve me, I will cause the Pharaoh of Egypt to be magically transported into Nubia, and there before the King and the people cause him to be beaten with five hundred blows. Then he would be returned to his own palace powerless." The third man then declared that if Amun would preserve him he would send a pestilence upon Egypt for the space of three years which would wither the crops and cause the cattle to weaken and die.

'Hearing these words, the King of Nubia rejoiced and called these sorcerers into his presence. "Which of you said that he had the power to cast a darkness across the skies of Egypt?" asked the King.

'"It was I Majesty, Heru, son of Tririt the sow," said the first in his oddly high-pitched voice.

'"And which of you may summon the Pharaoh of Egypt?" demanded the King.

'"It is I Lord, Heru son of Tnas-hit the negress," replied the second.

'"Then you must be the one who can cast a pestilence over Egypt," said the King.

'"That is so Majesty, for I am Heru son of Triphit the princess," declared the third.

'Then the King promised rich rewards to Heru, the son of Tnas-hit, and commanded him to fulfil his words. So the sorcerer constructed a litter of reeds complete with four bearers made of wax. He chanted magical formulae and breathed upon them so that they stirred into life.

"Go now to Egypt," cried Heru son of Tnas-hit, "lay hands upon the Pharaoh of that land and bring him back to me." At these words, the litter, wax bearers and all grew to human size and vanished.'

Here Se-Osiris paused and met the eye of the ragged ambassador. 'The curse of Amun-Ra and all the gods will fall upon you if you do not admit that all I have read is indeed set down within the sealed scroll.'

Defiantly the Nubian replied, 'These words are indeed written there.' A murmur of satisfaction was heard in the hall as Se-Osiris resumed the tale.

'All occurred as Heru, son of Tnas-hit the negress, had promised. The Pharaoh of Egypt was indeed borne by magical means to the land of Nubia, and once there was foully abused. Before the laughing King of that land and all his people the Pharaoh was forced to endure five hundred blows. Senseless, the bruised Pharaoh was then placed in the sorcerous litter and magically returned to his palace in far Egypt. Awakening, the Pharaoh cried out in pain. His attendants and slaves gathered about him as he recounted what to him was a terrible dream. They, thinking that the Pharaoh was afflicted with madness, spoke softly to ease his troubled mind. The King's chief magician Tehuti was summoned and when he saw the bloody bruises and welts which covered the Pharaoh's body he let out a great cry.

'"By the very life of Ptah, this is the work of dark sorcery that can only have come from the magicians of Nubia. Now I must make haste to protect the Pharaoh for he may again be abducted this night." Tehuti gathered his talismans, amulets and occult books. These he placed about the groaning Pharaoh's bed reciting hymns and spells all the while. Then Tehuti the chief magician took a boat to the temple of Thoth to pray that all evil be kept from his ailing lord. While engaged in prayer, the ibis-headed form of the god appeared to him to teach him the magic that would preserve the Pharaoh from all harm.

'The very next night, the sorcerers of Nubia attempted to renew their magical assault. But this time, the wax figures did not grow, neither did they journey to Egypt for the power of Thoth was stronger than theirs. Thus did Heru, son of Tnas-hit the negress, fail in his second attempt to humiliate the Pharaoh of Egypt.

'On the third night, the Pharaoh's magician Tehuti fashioned a magical litter of reeds, with four bearers made of wax. He now breathed upon them and recited spells bidding them to go to Nubia, to lay hands on the king of that land and to bear him into the land of Egypt. Speaking in one voice, the little figures promised to do all that their creator had asked. They at once grew to human size and were gone.'

Again, Se-Osiris paused in his recital. 'And is this, too, set down in the sealed scroll?' he asked. The Nubian ambassador, now less proud, replied that it was. Again Se-Osiris closed his eyes and began to read from the sealed scroll.

'Thus was the King of Nubia brought to the court of Egypt and there before the Pharaoh and all the assembled people was forced to endure five hundred blows. He was then returned by the magical litter to his own palace. Roaring with pain and anger, the Nubian king called for Heru, the son of Tnas-hit, demanding that he be protected from the wiles of the Egyptians. Yet Heru's arts could not prevent two further abductions and the Nubian king endured five hundred blows each time.

'After the third occasion, the Nubian king cursed Heru, son of Tnas-hit, swearing that the sorcerer would suffer an agonizingly slow death if he did not defeat the chief of the magicians of Egypt. Much troubled, Heru turned to his mother, the witch Tnas-hit, for advice. Woefully, Heru explained his predicament which caused his mother great anxiety.

'"My son," began the witch, "if you travel to Egypt to challenge this chief of magicians, then you will know only defeat. Therefore defy the King and do not go."

'"If only it were that simple," replied Heru, "for the King has assured me that I will suffer a long and agonizing death if I do not defeat the Egyptian."

'"Then let us devise a signal between us so that if you meet with disaster I will know of it and devise a way to help you," said Tnas-hit.

'Sorrowfully Heru replied, "Then, if I am vanquished, let all that you eat and drink turn to the colour of blood." With that, Heru left his mother to begin the long journey up the Nile to the capital of the Two Lands.

'Some time later Heru, son of Tnas-hit, came to the Hall of Audience of the Pharaoh, for he was a brave man despite his misgivings. With head held high he moved through the throngs of nobles and priests until he proudly stood before the Horus Throne itself. "Who among you has placed a wicked spell on the King of Nubia?" His voice rang out, silencing the assembly. Tehuti the chief magician came forth at once.

'"On the contrary, it is you who has worked evil against the Pharaoh."

'Now that his adversary was revealed Heru, son of Tnas-hit, muttered a potent spell causing a great flame to blaze fiercely in the centre of the hall. At this the crowd fell back and the Pharaoh cried out for the chief magician to save them all. His eyes fixed on those of the Nubian, Tehuti raised his hands and immediately a shower of rain began to fall, dousing the flames.

'Again Heru spoke a spell and a pitch darkness fell over the Hall of Audience so that none could see his neighbour nor his own hand before his face. This time Tehuti created a ball of light which dispelled the darkness utterly. Heru gathered his powers and again recited a spell of such venom that the hall was filled with swarm of insects whose buzzing inflicted deafness on all present. To answer this magical challenge, Tehuti summoned a flock of birds who swallowed each and every insect as they soared and dived about the high-pillared room.

'By now, the magical potency of Heru, son of Tnas-hit, was exhausted. He begged the Pharaoh for mercy and forgiveness, swearing by the names of all the gods that his magic would never trouble Egypt ever again. This oath satisfied both Pharaoh

130

and chief magician so Heru, son of Tnas-hit, was thrown
into a reed boat and sent down the Nile to his own land
a chastened and repentant man. Thus were the sorceries
of the Nubians overcome and all occurred as Tnas-hit
had said. She knew that disaster had befallen her son
when the wine in her cup turned to blood.'

The recitation of Se-Osiris had come to an end.
Opening his eyes, the boy met the gaze of the ragged
ambassador. 'Is all I have said true?'

'That it is,' replied the Nubian, 'though how you
have accomplished this feat I cannot say.'

'Then it is time that the truth was revealed,' replied
Se-Osiris in ringing tones. 'For, know this, I am the chief
magician Tehuti reborn to protect the Pharaoh and
the Two Lands of Egypt against the machinations of
the Nubians.'

The ambassador snarled, 'And I am that very Heru,
son of Tnas-hit, who, by the enchantments of my witch-
mother, has returned after five hundred years to work
my revenge.'

At this the court was filled with alarm as the ambassador,
ragged no longer, took on his true form of the powerful sorcerer. However, before he could speak a deadly spell Se-Osiris
called on the power of the gods of Egypt to undo the
Nubian's magic. At his words a mighty flame surged from the
earth about the feet of Heru. So fierce was the blaze that the
sorcerer was consumed utterly leaving behind not a charred
fragment of bone nor a scrap of ash.

When Ramesses the King, his son Khaemwaset and the
assembled nobles had recovered from this shock, they
looked about for Se-Osiris, but the boy, too, had vanished,
never to be seen again by any in the land of Egypt.

So, although the centuries old malice and cunning of
the evil Nubian sorcerer Heru had been vanquished, the
hearts of Khaemwaset and his wife Mahitouaskhit were
heavy for again they had lost a child. In time the princess
bore another son, whom Khaemwaset named as
Ousimanthor, and the pair were glad, but they never
forgot Se-Osiris and made many offerings to the divine
child that had once been theirs.

THE RAT OF MEMPHIS

N THE TIME WHEN THE TWO Lands of Egypt had known no darker days, there came to the Horus Throne one who had lately been a priest of wise Ptah, artificer of the gods. This new pharaoh did not forget his patron divinity and moved his court to Memphis, the holy seat of Ptah.

Now the Pharaoh Setnau, for such was his name, was a pious and devout worshipper who honoured the imperishable gods but had little knowledge of the ways of men. Thus the beginning of his reign was filled with festivals of rejoicing, and many sacrifices were made to the immortal powers, but Setnau paid no heed to the grumbling stomachs of his subjects or to the grumbling words of his armies.

No longer could the Pharaoh of Egypt style himself 'Lord of All the Lands' for the hosts of Assyria had risen and swept away the outposts of Egyptian sovereignty in the deserts of Syria, Judeah, Arabia and Edom. Again and again the armies of Egypt were overwhelmed by the might of Sennacherib, Great King of the Assyrians. Soon the forces of this mighty conqueror were on the very borders of Egypt itself and all the princes who had previously sent tribute to Pharaoh now made offerings to Sennacherib of Nineveh, master of Babylon, whose questing eyes fell upon the land of the Nile – for only Egypt remained free from his dominion.

The armies of the newly-crowned King Setnau were in a sorry state, for this neglectful Pharaoh had given them neither supplies

nor arms with which to repel the invading host. So, when the dust of the advance guard of Assyrian chariots was spied making for the northern city of Peluce, the bedraggled Egyptian soldiery were all for laying down their arms and surrendering themselves to the mercy of Sennacherib.

When Setnau was informed of this tragedy, he was filled with despair. He rose from the Horus Throne, set down the Crook and Flail of sovereignty and removed the Double Crown from his head. Then he wept, for he at last understood that his foolish policies had brought the once great kingdom of the Two Lands to the verge of ruin. Sadly, Setnau walked bare-headed to the temple of his god, the mighty Ptah. Prostrating himself before the god's image, Setnau prayed for all that day and for most of the following night. Then, exhausted, the King fell into a deep sleep at the embalmed feet of his god. And while he slept Setnau dreamed that Ptah stepped down from his place to comfort him.

'Do not fear my son,' said the god, 'for I am with you and by my power disaster may yet be averted.'

'But, Lord, my armies have deserted me, and the land of Egypt is defenceless against the terrible hordes of the King of Nineveh,' moaned Setnau.

'Even so,' replied Ptah, 'all will be well if you gather your personal guard, put on the Blue Crown of War and ride against the Assyrians.'

As soon as this was said, Setnau awoke to find himself sprawled on the granite floor of the temple, the softly smiling image of Ptah far above him.

His courage restored, Setnau hastened from the temple, calling for his men-at-arms to attend him. Clothing himself in the raiment of war, the Blue Crown set upon his head, and with less than two hundred men to follow him, Setnau mounted his chariot and prepared to face the might of Assyria. As his small procession marched through the streets of Memphis, labourers, merchants and shopkeepers came out with whatever weapon they could find and joined the soldiers who followed the King. In the countryside, too, peasants, cattle-herders and boatmen took what they could to defend their homes and country.

As swiftly as was possible this rag-tag army made its way across the wasteland to the more fertile region of Peluce, occupying the city and bolstering its meagre defences against the inevitable attack. Soon the uncounted thousands of Sennacherib's forces advanced to the very walls of the city. With the patient resolve and efficiency of a million ants they surrounded it, besieging the Pharaoh and his small force within.

To Setnau's surprise no word inviting his surrender came from the great encampment of Sennacherib. Neither did the Assyrians make any assault upon the city's walls. Instead, the invaders made camp fires and settled down for the night, confident that the defenders of Peluce could do nothing to dislodge them.

All that night Setnau paced the walls of Peluce pondering upon his own unwisdom in trusting to the word of Ptah, convinced that at the first light of dawn the hosts of Assyria would slay him and his force and then sweep down into the valley of the Nile. However, when the light of Ra filled the eastern sky, there was no attack. Instead there were cries of woe emerging from the Assyrian camp. At once, Setnau called for his chariots to issue forth from the city to engage his enemy.

As the gates opened, Setnau was amazed to see Assyrian warriors desperately trying to arm themselves only to find that the straps on their armour were chewed through. Similarly, archers found that the strings to their bows were gone and the charioteers discovered that the reins and tackle of their horses snapped in their hands.

Without hesitation, King Setnau urged his men forward and soon his small force had turned the tide of battle. The Assyrians abandoned their weapons and either fled from the scene or were slain where they stood. Of Sennacherib there was no sign save the dwindling dust cloud of his chariot as he made speed to safer territory.

Later, when all the invaders were dispersed or had fled, the Pharaoh Setnau sat upon a makeshift throne in a tent that had lately belonged to an Assyrian general. At that moment, his guards brought in a slave who prostrated himself before the

Pharaoh, begging for his life. Setnau ordered the man to rise and to tell his tale. Humbly the slave began.

'Great Pharaoh, last night when the army lay down to rest on the eve of battle, all within this mighty camp were confident of victory. The Assyrian lords knew that the Pharaoh of Egypt had but a small force and could not possibly hope to resist the might of the soldiers of Sennacherib.' At this, King Setnau nodded in agreement.

'But then,' continued the slave, 'there was a strange rustling in the undergrowth and rats of all shapes and sizes, from the fields, from the marshes, and from the irrigation canals, surged forth. They ran over sleeping men and between the feet of those who were awake. They infested the whole camp, chewing and nibbling here and there. No bowstring was safe from their gnawing teeth, no armour strap, no chariot tackle. Soon all that was left were shreds and scraps of leather. The Assyrian host numbered many thousands of men but we had no defence against an enemy such as this.' So saying, the slave bowed again. Setnau spared the man's life and gave the order that the camp of the Assyrians was to be looted before the return to Memphis.

Great was the triumphant welcome that Setnau and his men received on their entry to the city, but after the crowds had grown silent and his weary warriors had gone to their beds, Setnau went alone to the temple of Ptah to give thanks to the god whose army of rats had won the day. It was there in the temple that Setnau repented his previous neglect of the people and resolved to be a better ruler in future.

Thus it is that in the temple of Ptah stands a great stone statue of the smiling god bearing in his right hand the image of a humble rat. And upon the rat is written, 'Look upon me, for who beholds me, beholds the will of the god.'

135

THE SECULAR TALES

THE SECULAR TALES

THE SECULAR TALES comprise four charming folk stories which must have been told over and over, with ever-increasing elaboration, around camp fires and in villages the length of Egypt for centuries.

Though the stories generally culminate with a scene at the court of the Pharaoh, they are rarely historical in nature and reflect a view of the world more akin to that of fairy tales. In short, they are grounded in reality but will meander off into the fantastical and are, in effect, pure escapism.

The tale of 'The Shipwrecked Traveller' is a very tall tale indeed, reflecting a peasant's ignorance of foreign lands and a deep-seated dread of the sea. This last is an unsurprising attitude in a people who knew only a single river valley and the desert that lay beyond it. The land of Kush, which is the traveller's intended destination, must have been somewhere on the eastern coast of Africa but its exact location has been lost. Voyages to Kush were periodically undertaken from the Middle Kingdom onwards for it was from Kush that such luxuries as ivory and gold originated. The Ancient Egyptians had a sketchy knowledge of geography beyond their borders and often considered Nubia, their southern neighbour as Kushite territory. However, in this story Kush has left the realm of physical existence and entered that of fantasy, as indeed has Punt, another mysterious African region.

The story of 'The Eloquent Peasant' is a very old one, dating from the Ninth Dynasty. There are many versions of the story, four of which have been found complete on various papyrus documents. This must have been one of the most popular of Ancient Egyptian folk tales. The gaining of justice is the theme of the story, though it seems doubtful that the merry peasant had any thought of retribution or reward in mind. It is interesting to note that the peasant goes to great lengths to attract the notice of the judge implying that an equal-handed system of law was the exception rather than the rule in that period.

The tale of 'True and Lie' (or Maat and Gereg) deals with the rivalry of two brothers, the point of contention being the fate of a knife. The very names of the principal characters tell the reader where his sympathies should rest. The honest but unfortunate True was called Maat in the original text but was not meant to be confused with the goddess of the same name.

The story of 'The Treacherous Wife' is the subject matter of the d'Orbiney Papyrus in the British Museum. Its original owner, the Pharaoh Seti II, has had the kindness to imprint his name in hieroglyphics on the manuscript which was written by the scribe Anena. This was obviously a popular tale also featuring two brothers, Anpu and Bata. It, too, is a story of injustice and revenge, common themes running throughout Ancient Egyptian folklore. It has been suggested that the character of Bata (or Bitou) can be identified with the obscure Greek god Bitys who was introduced to Egypt during the Ptolemaic Period, while Anpu is none other than jackal-headed Anubis in disguise. Interestingly, these two deities had shrines on opposite banks of the Nile to each other and there was a well-known rivalry between them since the shrine of Anubis was considerably richer. Perhaps this is the origin of this entertaining tale.

THE SHIPWRECKED TRAVELLER

THERE ONCE CAME TO THE court of Pharaoh a bedraggled stranger who waited at the gate to beg an audience with the Lord of the Two Lands. When his turn was come he bowed and humbly asked the guardian of the portal to allow him admittance, but the gatekeeper refused, thinking that the mighty King would be offended at the sight of such a raggedly dressed oaf.

'But I have a tale of marvels to convey to the King's majesty,' protested the man.

'Then you will tell me this tale, that I may judge whether the Pharaoh would receive you,' responded the guardian of the gate.

Sighing, the stranger settled himself in the dust and began his story: 'Though now I appear nought but a ragged peasant, I am a nobleman who was destined to be an overseer of the King's mines in distant Kush. To this end I took ship upon the Sea of Reeds even though I felt as much fear of the endless seas as was possible. But I contented myself with the thought that the ship was sturdy, being one hundred and fifty cubits long and forty cubits wide. No less than one hundred of the finest mariners in all of Pharaoh's dominions made up its crew. Their hearts were those of lions and there was no tempest or other peril of the deeps that afrighted them. But the gods of the wind did not smile on us for, as soon as we had left the Sea of Reeds and dared to venture on to the awesome vastness of the ocean, a dreadful storm came upon us. The mighty waves lashed against the ship. The gales howled about our sails and men were swept from their posts to die in the bottomless depths. Though our commander was valiant and wise in the ways of the elements, the sea had no mercy or remorse. Soon our ship was crushed by the pounding of the waves. The winds ripped down the rigging and tore the oars from the numbed hands of our hapless mariners whose bravery now availed them not as our vessel floundered.

'I alone survived that terrible night for I had the good fortune to seize upon a fallen timber which buoyed me up as my companions sank from sight. For three days

I drifted alone upon the bosom of the endless ocean until, by happy chance, I was cast up upon an island and thus was saved my life. I lay gasping for breath, my body torn by pangs of gnawing hunger. When I had somewhat recovered my strength I gazed about me to see that this was a fertile isle indeed. Here were many bushes bearing grapes and figs. All around were melons, berries and grain. The streams were filled with life. Succulent fish abounded as did plump birds. In this place I knew that at least I would not starve. I fortified myself with figs and then gave thanks to all the gods for my deliverance.

'Contented and strengthened, I resolved to explore the island when all at once a mighty clamour arose which first I took to be another tempest. The trees shook and the earth quaked beneath my feet as a monstrous serpent reared above me. Glorious and fearful was the sight, for this gargantuan reptile was more than thirty cubits in length. Its vast back was covered in golden scales, each one the size of a man's hand, while its belly was the translucent blue of lapis lazuli. From its chin grew the likeness of a kingly beard of two cubits' length, but more terrifying than all were its eyes, the vertical slits of which had all the glimmering of intelligence. Again in fear of my life I fell to my knees as the creature's booming voice echoed across the isle.

'"Little one," the serpent began, "what has brought you to my kingdom? Speak swiftly but be warned for, if you do not acquaint me with anything which I have not heard before or knew not before, then will you fill my belly."

'So saying, the monster seized me in its powerful jaws and bore me to its lair where it released me and fixed me again with a glare. I felt as helpless as a bird enchanted by the eyes of a cobra. I could not move yet at length I summoned the will to speak. My voice trembling, I told the kingly serpent of my voyage to Kush, of the disaster that had befallen me and of my drowned comrades. On hearing this, the mighty serpent grew compassionate.

'"Be of good cheer my poor mariner and be not afraid, for the benevolence of the gods has delivered you to my peaceful realm. This is a blessed island where nothing is wanting. All good things are here. There is food and water, the air is pure and no noxious insects plague the happy inhabitants. I am the king of this place and, like all my kind, have the power of prophecy. Therefore I can tell you that you are not forsaken and that when the moon has waxed and waned four times a ship will come to bear you homeward."

'Weeping with gratitude I thanked the serpent. "When I return to my home I will go to the Pharaoh and tell him of your generosity," I declared. "After this I will again take ship and return to you with offerings of costly incense, perfumes and sacred oils to honour you like a god. I will slay asses as a sacrifice, pluck the feathers from birds to make you a fine robe and bring my personal fortune here as a gift to my saviour."

'At this the serpent gave a rumbling laugh. "Do not tell me that you are rich in perfumes and fine goods for I know that all Egypt has is incense of an ordinary sort. I am the Prince of Punt and possess as much sweet-smelling perfume as I require. As for wealth, I have all that I am ever likely to need, nor have I any use for a robe or the deaths of asses. Furthermore, my isle is hidden from mortal sight and when you depart from it you will never see it again. So, be content to dwell with me a while, to discourse with me and simply to savour the pleasure of living."

'For many days I walked next to the gorgeous slithering monarch talking of this and that, of the ways of beast and man, of the courses of the stars and of the mysteries of land and sea. The serpent told me that the isle was inhabited by his kinsfolk, serpents all to the number of seventy-five, of various ages, who were equally inclined to philosophy and had a distaste for human flesh.

'The moon waxed and waned four times before a ship approached as my host had prophesied. I, however, was cautious and climbed a tree the better to observe what manner of company crewed the vessel. It was with joy that I perceived this ship flew the banner of Horus. Keeping out of sight of the newly arrived visitors, the kingly serpent bade me farewell and gave me many gifts of precious perfumes, ivory tusks, cassia, kohl, sweet woods, apes and baboons, gold and silver.

'"Goodbye little friend," said the serpent sadly. "In two months you will see your wife and family again, but I doubt that you will ever forget me." He then slithered off into the dense undergrowth and I have not seen him from that day to this.

'The crew greeted me as though I were a long-lost brother, stowing my cargo with their own. Then we set sail as I stood in the stern watching the mysterious isle of the serpent king fade as does a dream on waking. And here I am at the gates of the palace for, though I am roughly dressed, the ship yonder bears all the wealth that the kingly serpent gave me, and these things I would offer up to Pharaoh.'

In wonderment, the guardian of the gate ushered the traveller within the palace to the presence of the Pharaoh. There the stranger again recounted his tale. So pleased was the Lord of the Two Lands with the story that he rewarded the adventurer with many ranks and titles and allowed him to retain the revenues of his voyage and all the gifts that the serpent king had given him. Then did the noble traveller return to his home weighed down by his new-found wealth and position. Thus ends the tale of the shipwrecked traveller.

THE ELOQUENT PEASANT

FAR TO THE NORTH, IN the delta near to the Great Green Sea, there lived a peasant with his family. Though poor, these simple people were happy and lived each day with joy. Much of the reason for this was that the peasant was a clever fellow with always a merry quip or story to lighten the load of unrelenting drudgery that was the lot of himself and his kin.

Now, much of this peasant's meagre income came from trading in salt and rushes which he daily took to the nearby town of Henen-seten, returning at nightfall with supplies. Then would his wife and children rejoice for the peasant always had some tale to tell of his adventures in what they considered to be a mighty city.

It happened that in order to get to the town the merry peasant had to pass close to the Nile through lands which belonged to the powerful house of Fefa. Often, when he was upon this route, he would encounter an ill-favoured and ill-natured tenant-farmer in the service of that great house. His name was Tehuti-nekht, son of Asri. Over the course of time this Tehuti-nekht, who had no thought for the benefit or comfort of anyone save himself, had expanded his plot of land nearer and nearer to the banks of the Nile. Thus, it became more and more difficult to pass without setting foot upon the territory of Fefa.

One day Tehuti-nekht saw the merry peasant approach, leading several asses burdened with bags of salt and papyrus rushes of the finest quality suitable for making parchment. At this sight his covetous heart urged upon him a scheme to dispoil the peasant of his goods. Tehuti-nekht took a fine shawl and spread it upon the ground so that one edge was within the barley which marked the boundary of his land, while the other stretched down to the waters of the sacred Nile.

The happy peasant sang as he came on his way. As he drew near Tehuti-nekht shouted at him. 'Stop! Surely you do not intend to drive your foul-smelling, muddy-footed beasts over my fine shawl?'

142

'I will endeavour to avoid it good sir,' replied the peasant, laughing. At this, see-ing that the Nile way was impassable, he led his docile beasts into the field of barley. Then Tehuti-nekht shouted again.

'See how your asses ruin my crop.'

'This is a misfortune but, as you can see, there is no other way,' answered the peas-ant, still smiling. Wrathfully Tehuti-nekht strode towards the peasant's little caravan.

'Look how the lead ass is eating my barley. I claim the beast as compensation for the theft.' The farmer then took hold of the rope which guided the beast and marched off with it, the ass following, and all the other asses following that.

Now the peasant wrung his hands in despair. 'Are you nought but a robber then? Am I to be dispoiled of my goods within the lands of Fefa? Be fearful O Tehuti-nekht for I shall go to the high steward Meruitensa, and bring my complaint before him.'

At this Tehuti-nekht paused. Turning, he laughed scornfully. 'And do you think that the exalted will listen to one such as you, a mere peasant? Who will worry about your woes? On this land I am the very hand of the lord steward Meruitensa.' So say-ing, he took a stick and beat the poor peasant before marching his prizes away.

The next day the peasant returned to plead with Tehuti-nekht who had stolen all he had. From dawn until dusk did the man beg but Tehuti-nekht had a heart of gran-ite and bade him hold his tongue, threatening to kill him if he did not obey.

It was with a heavy heart and little hope that the sad peasant presented himself at the fine house of the high steward Meruitensa. On his arrival he found the lord preparing to embark on a voyage. Bowing to the dust the peasant nervously spoke of the ill that had been done to him and begged for the steward to send one of his attendants to hear the case. With a gesture of the fingers, the high steward handed the matter to a scribe, who questioned the peasant in detail. With a tongue like quicksilver the peasant told of all that had befallen him, of the encroachment of the common land near the Nile, of the cunning and cruelty of Tehuti-nekht and of the theft of his property. Impressed with his eloquence, the scribe hastened after his master for he was of the opinion that this was a matter worthy of law.

So the matter came to judgement and the ragged peasant stood before the jewelled splendour that was the high steward Meruitensa. 'Let this fellow bring forth a witness,' said the high steward not deign-ing to address the peasant directly, 'for, if this case be proven, it may be necessary to beat Tehuti-nekht or cause him to pay some trifle in compensation.'

143

'Great Lord, flower of justice, mightiest of the mighty, guide of the needy, who acts as the provider to the widow, father of orphans, protector of the helpless,' said the peasant, 'I am but a poor man who has been deprived of those few possessions which I did once own. Alas I have no witness to this crime which has brought me to beggary, yet there are many who could testify to my hard work and efforts to provide for my family. There are many who could testify that I have always abided by the law and honoured yourself, the Pharaoh and the gods. Surely you cannot take the word of an ill-tempered and greedy oaf such as Tehuti-nekht above my own, even though this villain is a gentleman farmer while I am but a humble peasant.'

Despite himself the high steward was intrigued by this loquacious peasant and marvelled that one with so little education could compose and deliver a speech of such force and passion in surroundings which would have made most men of his class quake. Aside from this, he was quite flattered by the man's description of him, which closely tallied with his own opinion. Now, though rightness and justice were on the side of peasant, the lord steward did not wish to condemn Tehuti-nekht, for by doing so he would offend all tenant farmers who worked his land. Thus, in order to delay the verdict, he ruled that he would consult with the wisest of the wise and that the peasant should come again another day to present his case once more.

That evening, the high steward wrote to the Pharaoh Nebkanra saying: 'O Lord of the Two Lands, there has come before me a peasant whose goods have been stolen. He is of such eloquence and persuasiveness that I marvel for surely the gods themselves have touched him. Tell me, Majesty, what should I do with him?'

In due time a reply was received: 'Faithful servant, do not answer him yet, but have his speeches set down and brought to me. Furthermore, see that his family is provided for, but do not tell him who commands this bounty.' As the Pharaoh had written so was it done and each day as the peasant again spoke his case, with more and more florid details, every word was set down by scribes and a copy sent to His Majesty. Each night a messenger came to the peasant's hovel with such quantities of bread, meat and beer that the poor family had never before dined so well.

At length the high steward Meruitensa became heartily bored with the constant complaint of the eloquent peasant. So, when next he came, the lord would not receive him. The peasant then stood beneath Meruitensa's window and again recited his plea. These speeches continued even when the steward ordered the peasant beaten for presumption. Finally, his ears deafened by the sweetness of the peasant's words, his will broken by the fellow's determination and command of politics, and defeated by his honesty, the lord high steward Meruitensa sent two guards to the humble fellow's house. At first the peasant and his family were frightened for they feared that they would now all be beaten or thrown to the sacred crocodiles, but they were summoned to appear before the Pharaoh himself in the capital far away.

In the very barge of Meruitensa the wide-eyed little clan travelled down the Nile. Each day brought new wonders: the mighty cliffs, the endless extent of the cultivated land, marvellous cities and fleets of boats upon the river, and not least the glory of the pyramids themselves. Even more wondrous was the palace of the Pharaoh itself which loomed above them, seeming to touch the sky.

So it was that the peasant and his family were brought before the awesome glory of Nebkanra, King of Upper and Lower Egypt. They threw themselves upon the ground only to be raised by the powerful hand of the Pharaoh himself.

'I count you as a friend, my good fellow,' said the King smiling, 'for I have been wondrously entertained by your speeches to my steward. Your goodness and honesty shine from your words like the light of my father Ra.' Gaping with astonishment, the peasant's eloquence failed him for once. The Pharaoh continued. 'I particularly liked the way in which you played on the high steward's pomposity. It made amusing reading. I therefore decree that you will be raised to the rank of gentleman, that the property of that villain Tehuti-nekht shall be stripped from him and given to you. Furthermore, you will be my overseer and administer my estates in the North and riches are to be your portion.'

Thus did the eloquent peasant become a trusted minister of the Lord of the Two Lands, and was greatly honoured by him.

TRUE AND LIE

IN THE TIME WHEN THE NINE gods of Heliopolis ruled the land and great Ra was a mortal pharaoh there lived two brothers as unalike as sea and sand, as fire and water, as day and night. The first was handsome, good and kind. Justice and the ways of Maat were in his very being, so all named him True. His envious brother did not have the looks of True, but was stunted and warped in his nature. His heart was black and justice was unknown to him. For this reason all called him Lie.

One day, True found himself lacking a knife so respectfully requested the loan of a blade from his brother. Grudgingly Lie handed over the weapon and no more was said. Now it is a fact that all have faults no matter how good they might be, and this was the case with True for, though he had no malice, he tended to be absent-minded. So, when the day's tasks were done True was alarmed to discover that he had mislaid his brother's knife.

With copious apologies True begged his brother's forgiveness, promising to replace the lost knife with one of his own. To this suggestion the wicked Lie replied contemptuously, 'The knife was unique. Its blade contained the rarest metals to be found in the deep mines of the mountain of El, its handle was fashioned from the hardest wood of Koptos, its sheath had the likeness of the tomb of a god, while its leather thongs originated from the cattle of Kar.'

'But … that is not my memory of the blade,' said True innocently.

'Nevertheless that is my claim,' insisted Lie, 'and if you do not replace the knife with one equally as fine and rare I demand a legal judgement.'

Poor True was at a loss for there was nothing he could say or do to dissuade his brother.

So the arrogant Lie and the downhearted True came before the court of the Nine Gods at Heliopolis. With no trace of shame Lie made his outrageous claims, while True had nothing to say for he could not conceive that his brother would tell such an outrageous falsehood. Now, since True offered no defence, the gods found in favour of Lie and asked him what punishment should be meted out to one who had deprived him of such a valuable object. 'Let his eyes be struck from his head, let all his property be given to me and let him be made the doorkeeper of my house as compensation,' demanded the triumphant Lie.

The harsh sentence was swiftly carried out, for even then True did not protest. He was led back to Lie's house there to sit in the dust at the gate to listen for intruders. However, it was not long before the sight of his maimed brother began to trouble Lie and he was afflicted by the unaccustomed sensation of guilt. Finding this hard to bear he ordered two servants who had previously served True to take their former master to the lair of a pride of lions where he would be instantly killed.

It was with heavy hearts that the two led True away from the gate for they were sad that so terrible an end was to befall their former master. Together, they decided that they would not do as Lie had wished but abandon True in the rugged mountains far away from Lie's domain with some food and water. There, by the mercy of the gods, some kind traveller might take pity on True and lead him to safety.

Alone on a rocky hillside, True wandered helpless and blind. His meagre rations were soon exhausted and, abandoning hope, he lay down beneath an outcrop of rock hoping that death would come swiftly. But the will of the gods is strange and this was not to be True's fate for soon a great lady and her entourage

passed by. The lady was immediately taken by the remarkable beauty of the distressed wretch and sent her servants to help him. True accompanied the party to her house where he was bathed, given food and drink and given comfortable quarters near to the gateway, for it was this lady's intention that True should act as her gatekeeper henceforth. However, this was not her only desire, for blind though he was, True was the most handsome man that she had ever seen.

It was not long before the humble gatekeeper True shared the bed of the great lady of the house returning to his post before daybreak so that none would know of their secret. In the fullness of time the lady grew great with child and eventually gave birth to a son who was as handsome and good as his unknown father. Years passed and all went well with them. True still sat at the gate during the day but in the darkness of the night he found his way to his mistress's bed far better than could any seeing man. Their son prospered and grew strong in body, his learning excelling any of his classmates, and his beauty surpassing all save that of the gatekeeper True.

There was only one thing that marred this blessed boy's life and that was the taunts of his companions who mocked him asking, 'Who is your father, clever one?' He turned to his mother for help, 'Tell me the identity of my father which you have concealed for so long,' he begged.

Yielding to his pleas the lady pointed at the gate, 'There sits your father, the good-hearted True whom I would marry were we of the same rank,' she said sadly.

'Marriage or not,' cried the boy, 'it is not fitting that my father should sit so like a servant at the gate.' With that he leapt to his feet and, despite his father's protests, the boy brought True into the house, arrayed him in fine garments and placed him on the high seat with a stool beneath his feet. Then he hailed True as the master of the estate, while his mother was proud that her son showed a courage that over-turned convention. A great feast was held that night to show the world that True was the lady's husband in all but name.

Some days later, True's son came to his father with a question, 'Tell me, honoured sire, who brought you to the sad state of a blind servant, when it is evident that you are of gentle birth?'

At this, True sighed and related the sad tale of Lie's betrayal. When he had finished, the boy raged, 'Is there no justice in this world? Fear not father, for I will see to it that right is done.' With these words the boy put on new sandals, fastened a sword to his belt, took ten loaves from the kitchen, picked up a staff and a water-skin and made for the cattle herd that belonged to his mother. Choosing a particularly fine ox, the boy led it away towards the estate of Lie, beyond the mountain.

On reaching the outskirts of Lie's pastures, the boy sought out the chief herdsman of the cattle. Sitting down with him, the boy shared his loaves and engaged him in conversation. After they had spoken for a while, the boy confided, 'I have a problem which you may be able to help me solve.'

'I will help if I can young sir,' replied the herdsman, 'for you seem a decent sort.'

'My problem is this,' continued the son of True, 'I have to go into the town for several days and cannot take this fine ox with me. Therefore will you keep the beast with your herd and tend it for me until my return?'

'That I will,' agreed the herdsman, 'but what will you give me for this service?'

'All the things that I carry,' cheerfully replied the boy. So when the herdsman had taken the loaves, water-skin, staff, good sandals and sword, and the fine ox was min-gled with Lie's cattle the boy departed, whistling, towards the town.

A day or two later Lie came to his pastures to choose an ox for a feast. On seeing the fine ox that the boy had brought he summoned his herdsman. 'I will take that one with me, for it is a splendid animal with much flesh upon its bones.'

'Begging your pardon, Lord,' said the herdsman humbly, 'I cannot release this particular beast for it is not one of your own. Choose another I beg, for to slaugh-ter this one would break a binding promise.'

'Insolent wretch,' shouted Lie. 'That one I have chosen and that one I will have. When its owner returns allow him to pick another from my herd.' Reluctantly the man agreed and the ox was led away for slaughter.

The following day True's son returned from the town. 'Where is the fine ox that I left with you?' he asked the herdsman.

'Alas my boy, my master Lie has taken it for a feast, but has said that you may have the pick of his cattle to take as your own in recompense.'

'This is outrageous,' shouted the boy, 'for none of this sorry herd are a match for my fine animal. Where is there an ox amongst these so large that if it were to stand in Heliopolis its tail would reach the delta as mine would? Where is the ox whose horns would over-spread the Nile so that the tip of one horn would touch the east-ern hills while the other would touch the western hills as mine could do?'

The herdsman was astonished by the boy's words as he led him before his master. Again the young man spoke of the wondrous animal that had been taken and the meagre recompense that had been offered.

'That is not my memory of your ox,' Lie protested.

'Nevertheless, these are the facts of the case and I will take you to law,' said the young man stubbornly. So it was that the son of True journeyed to Heliopolis to lay charges against Lie before the Nine Gods.

In the presence of the Great Ones, the son of True again stated his case against Lie. He described in detail the mighty girth and attributes of his marvellous ox and accused Lie of theft. The gods muttered amongst themselves finally addressing the boy, 'Surely you are mistaken concerning the fine qualities of your lost animal, for we have never seen an ox as big as that.'

The boy's eyes narrowed as he rejoined, 'And where then O gods have you seen a knife with a blade made of the rarest metals from the deepest mines of the moun-tain of El? Where a blade whose handle is made of the most expensive woods of Koptos? What weapon has thongs originating from the fabled herds of Kar? And what implement has ever had a sheath resembling the magnificence of the tomb of a god? Judge therefore between True and Lie once more, for I am the son of True, and I have come to avenge the wrong that has been done to him.'

The gods, who forgot nothing, now turned their august attention to Lie regarding him quizzically. 'As Amun-Ra and the Pharaoh endure,' said Lie, 'if True still lives then let me suffer the fate to which once I condemned him.' For Lie was sure that True had been devoured by lions long ago.

The young man laughed then. 'Indeed as Amun-Ra and the Pharaoh endure, if True be found alive then let Lie suffer even as he suffered. Let him be beaten and mistreated, let him be blinded and his property seized. Let him be made to serve as gatekeeper to the living True.'

To this the gods agreed and a messenger was sent to the great lady's house to bring True to Heliopolis. The horrified Lie saw his blinded brother arrive in great state before he was dragged off to have his eyes struck from his head.

True was given the estates of Lie; those which he had stolen by falsehood and those which he had possessed previously. Again was True raised to his former rank and thus was married to the great lady. Finally, the gods, who felt somewhat guilty, restored his sight and renewed the youthfulness of both him and his wife. As for True's son, the gods gave him the name of Loyal and bestowed on him the lands of his mother which he held until both his parents had departed to the west, whereupon he became the richest man in the Two Lands. Lie, spent the rest of his miserable days as a blind gatekeeper. Thus ends the salutary tale of the brothers True and Lie.

ANIMAL WORSHIP

TO THE ANCIENT Egyptian mind, animals were the worldly manifestation of a godly essence. That is to say that, just as the individual gods had characteristics, certain animals would share in these and thereby take on a portion of the nature of that god. Anubis, god of mummification and protector of cemeteries, is portrayed as a jackal or as a jackal-headed man because jackals were known to haunt graveyards. Therefore the association between the two was born.

The cat-goddess Bast was regarded as a huntress as well as the fickle patroness of lovers. The former association is self-explanatory, the latter because, though a cat is soft, affectionate and beautiful, it also has claws, and love can hurt and indeed leave deep scars. Similarly the wise Thoth is identified with the precision of the probing beak of the ibis as well as the impertinent curiosity of the baboon. Solar gods like Ra and Horus have falcon attributes, keen eyesight and the ability to hover for long periods, as does the sun.

The same logical process can be applied to most of the gods of the Ancient Egyptians. The animals associated with these divinities often provided the banners and symbols of a particular area and were thought to express something of the nature of the inhabitants. This practice is still common today, as the lion of England and Scotland, the eagle of the USA, the dragon of Wales and the rooster of France, among many others, will attest.

THE TREACHEROUS WIFE

LONG AGO TWO BROTHERS, Anpu and Bata by name, tilled the land close by the shore of the sacred Nile. Anpu was the wealthier, for he was the eldest and had inherited the property of their father; the cattle, crops and home. Bata, the younger, was contented and worked as a labourer on the farm. So good-natured was Bata that the beasts of the fields and the birds of the air took him to their hearts and over the years he learned to understand their tongues.

In time, Anpu took a wife, a beautiful girl with flashing eyes and aristocratic bearing. With her he lived in the house, while his brother Bata happily moved his few belongings into the barn.

While toiling in the fields one day Anpu, whose foresight was not what it should be, realized that he had forgotten the seed corn. Shouting to Bata he told the lad to run and fetch it. Swiftly the boy came to the house to find his sister-in-law sitting at the door. 'Oh Bata,' she murmured, 'would you not like to sit here with me?'

'That I would, but your husband calls me from the field,' replied Bata innocently.

'You should not listen to what Anpu says,' replied the seductress, 'for he is a fool and you are the better man.' Bata's face reddened as he pushed past her and into the house. When he returned with the seed corn, the wife stood barring his way, 'Oh Bata, forget Anpu and lie with me.' Bata was at a loss and roughly pushed the woman away and ran back to the field.

Anpu saw his brother's flushed looks yet did not comment, thinking they were caused by Bata's speedy return. Later, when the two returned from their labours, they were horrified to discover Anpu's wife lying on the ground moaning, her clothes torn and her hair in disarray. 'Who has done this?' demanded Anpu.

'I cannot tell you husband,' replied his wife whimpering. At this Bata sought to lend assistance, but the cunning girl drew back as if in fear. On seeing this, Anpu's face grew dark with rage for he now believed that Bata had assaulted his wife.

All night Anpu lay wide-eyed and sleepless next to his beloved wife who moaned and wept in the darkness. Anpu spoke in the unseeing night, 'Now will you tell me who has attacked you?'

His wife sobbed as she replied, 'It was none other than Bata your brother who demanded my favours. I refused him with harsh words and reminded him that just as you the elder brother are like a father to him, I as your wife am like a mother but he heeded not. Then he beat me to keep me silent. If you allow him to live then I shall surely kill myself so great is my shame.' It was then that Anpu decided that he must be revenged upon his brother and resolved to kill him.

As the light of Ra filled the world Bata awoke and set out for the fields. As he departed, Anpu took a long butcher's knife and placed it in his pack. He then followed in pursuit of his brother. Bata sang as he walked, yet his merry song was stilled as a bird flew close crying: 'Beware, beware.'

What could have disturbed the creature so,' wondered the innocent Bata. Passing some cattle he noticed that they regarded him with sombre eyes. Deeply they lowed: 'Beware of Anpu, O Bata.' Frightened now, Bata's pace had become a run as the voices of the animals spoke in unison, 'Your brother Anpu means to murder you, beware.'

A rustling in the reeds warned Bata of his brother's presence. Fear gave his feet wings as he fled the knife-wielding enemy who once he had loved. It was not long before the rage of Anpu had matched the terror of Bata and both were breathless as they continued the pursuit. But all was not lost for Bata; for, far above the all-seeing eye of Ra observed them and the might of the sun-god was sent forth to part the two. At once a stream bubbled through the undergrowth as a crocodile-infested portion of the Nile swept between the brothers so that Anpu could not cross. Knowing that he was now safe Bata fell to his knees in exhaustion, giving thanks for his deliverance, while Anpu on the opposite bank screamed with impotent rage.

When Bata had recovered his breath he called to Anpu across the stream, 'Brother why do you wish to kill me?'

In fury Anpu replied, 'For the foul dishonour you have done to my wife.'

'But I have done no dishonour, even though she tempted me when I went to the house for seed corn,' protested Bata.

'You deny that you have assaulted my beloved wife?' shouted the elder brother.

'That I do and swear it before all the gods. Why else would Ra raise a stream between us to prevent your lawful vengeance?'

Anpu was silent at this. He thought for a long time and his murderous passion weakened even as the stream between them now started to ebb.

Repenting of his hasty actions Anpu threw his knife to his brother to prove that he had lost his murderous intent and shouted to Bata, 'Let us now return to our home.'

'Pardon brother,' replied Bata, 'but what you have done to harm me has been done at the behest of a whore. Why did you pursue me before you had heard my story? I will not set foot in your house again but go to the Vale of Acacia, for I fear the wiles of your wife.' Bata then picked up his brother's knife and cut off his own penis which he threw into the stream where a fish swallowed it. Bata fell fainting to the ground as Anpu stood helpless on the farther shore wringing his hands.

Weakly Bata spoke, 'I will depart now for the Vale of Acacia, safely hidden there I will enchant my heart to dwell in the topmost branch of an acacia tree and thus my life will be preserved. If it falls then come and seek for it and continue your search no matter how long it takes you. When you find my heart place it in water and it will revive and take vengeance for me. You will know when my heart falls when the beer in your cup foams and overflows. When this happens come at once.' So saying, the bleeding Bata turned his back on his brother and set his face towards the blessed vale there to make his home.

Moaning with inner pain Anpu returned to his house to find his triumphant wife smiling. Without a word Anpu took up a spear and ran her through at once. He then threw her body to the wild beasts and dwelt in mourning for his lost brother from that day forth. But all was not yet done, for the soul of the whore-wife was restless and longed for a new body to make her own.

In the mean time Bata dwelt happily in the Vale of Acacia, hunting and fishing. True to his word he enchanted his heart and set it in the topmost bough of a tree.

One day, the nine great gods were walking beneath the shady lushness of the vale. Bata, coming upon them, threw himself to the ground, bowing his head to the earth. In kindly tones the gods told him of what his brother Anpu had done for they were sorry for the brothers and knew that a great injustice had occurred. Then did Ra, the light of the two horizons instruct ram-headed Khnum to fashion a woman upon his potter's wheel, to be Bata's wife and comfort him. But cow-eyed Hathor, in her seven-fold form as the goddess of fate, warned that such a one would be ill-omened and misfortune's favourite.

Khnum, lord of the source of life, did as he had been bidden and soon an incomparably lovely girl named Bintnefer or 'Daughter of gods', walked in the Vale of

Acacia. As soon as Bata laid eyes on her he fell in love and the two dwelt, chaste but happy in that blessed land for a long while. So greatly did Bata love Bintnefer that he cautioned, 'Oh my love, never leave this vale and be particularly wary of the deep green sea for I am a eunuch and cannot do those things a man could do to protect his wife.' Then he told her of his heart which still nested high in the acacia tree adding, 'If any should find my heart then I would have to fight with him.'

Now Bintnefer was a wilful girl, for the soul that had previously belonged to Anpu's wife had found a new home in her, and she did not heed Bata's words, so each day while her eunuch husband hunted, she walked on the sea-shore. So lovely was she that the very sea itself fell in love with her and longed for some token. So the sea persuaded the acacia tree to snatch a lock of the lady's hair when next she came.

And so, when Bintnefer next walked on the sea-shore the acacia tree reached down a twig and took a lock of her fragrant hair, tossing it into the waves. The waters embraced this lock for a while, but the sea is fickle and eventually forgot Bintnefer and deposited her hair at the very spot where the Pharaoh's laundresses washed the royal linens. Now because Bintnefer had been made by the hand of a god her very essence had an odour of perfume. Her hair retained this virtue and passed it on to the Pharaoh's clothes.

When the servants of the Lord of the Two Lands smelled this heavy fragrance they complained to the laundresses, who could not explain it. This mystery continued for many days until the chief laundress discovered the scented lock of hair on the shore. She took it to Pharaoh who was intrigued by this wonder. Summoning his wise men the Pharaoh asked them to explain. The sages stroked their beards and muttered, 'This hair belongs to a daughter of the gods, whose perfumed essence fills her body. It is our opinion that this is a gift from the eternal ones and that this lady is destined to be your wife.'

By command of the Pharaoh messengers were sent to all the lands to find this fragrant lady. Months passed and all returned save those who had gone to the Vale of Acacia. The reason for their disappearance was this: as Bintnefer had seen each messenger she had recognized that each was a true man, and to each she had revealed the secret of Bata's heart. Each one, in turn, had found the heart and been challenged to a duel by Bata who, although he was a eunuch, had defeated and slain them all.

The patience of the Pharaoh was now exhausted so he came in person to the vale accompanied by a battalion of soldiers. In anticipation of more gentle meetings, he also brought a company of women with them bearing gifts of jewellery and garments to woo his future bride.

As chance would have it the Pharaoh encountered Bintnefer in the shade of the very tree which harboured Bata's heart. As soon as Bintnefer saw the King her heart, which had been dormant, knew love. The Pharaoh took her in his arms kissing her passionately. 'My Lord,' gasped Bintnefer, 'my husband, though a eunuch, is a fearsome foe, but he has a weakness. If you will instruct your guards to cut down this tree, and break up its wood into splinters then there will be nothing to fear.'

As she had spoken so it was done. The acacia tree was felled and, far away, the hunting Bata fell stone dead as the tree crashed to the ground. However, this did not concern either the Pharaoh or his new bride for they returned in triumph to Egypt and were happy one with another.

Now Anpu, Bata's elder brother, had dwelt morosely at his farm for no less than seven years. On the very day that Bata died the beer in his cup frothed and flowed over the rim. 'This is the day that Bata foretold,' said Anpu, immediately setting off towards the Vale of Acacia to retrieve his brother's hidden heart. Arriving at the vale, Anpu wept to see his brother's corpse, cold and lifeless on the ground. He tended it and laid it out as was the custom, then he looked for the hiding place of the heart.

Long did he search but nowhere could he find the acacia tree. After three long years Anpu sadly decided that his quest was in vain and made ready to return to his home. 'I will look again one more time as I pass through this vale,' said Anpu to himself. No sooner did he say this than he saw an acacia berry lying on the ground. Some instinct told Anpu that this was no ordinary fruit but the very heart of his dead brother concealed by magic. He took the berry and immersed it in a jar of fresh water and lay down to sleep. During that night the berry drank in all the fluid becoming a heart once more. Carefully Anpu lifted it and put it back into his brother's cold body. As soon as this was done Bata's eyelids flickered and he breathed once more. But, as he did so, the body of Bata began to change until it was transformed into a young bull covered with strange markings. Speaking with the voice of a man the bull-Bata said, 'Now is the time for vengeance. Ride upon my back O Anpu and we shall go to the court of the Pharaoh himself, where you will be rewarded for bringing such a marvel as myself to the King's notice.'

Some days later news was brought to the Lord of the Two Lands that a man riding on the back of a wondrous bull had entered the city. The Pharaoh believed the beast to be the Bull of Meroe, an incarnation of the soul of Amun and therefore an excellent omen. He rewarded Anpu with much gold and sent him back to his farm. The bull-Bata was given apartments adjoining the palace, was dressed in the finest linens and bedecked with gold. Curiosity about this bull spread around the court like a desert wind, so it was not long before Bintnefer, the royal favourite, came to see the beast. As she bent to stroke its forehead the bull spoke softly to her alone, 'See faithless one, I still live.'

Shocked, Bintnefer asked, 'Who are you?'

'I am Bata. I know how you felled the acacia tree to be rid of me, yet still I live.'

Terrified, Bintnefer fled to the Pharaoh composing herself as she did so. When she arrived in his presence Bintnefer sat next to him and caressed his thigh. 'O my lord, pray grant whatever I may ask of you,' she cooed.

'Ask whatever you wish my love,' he replied, 'for all in my kingdom is yours.'

'I wish to eat the liver of the bull who is the soul of Amun,' she demanded.

'No girl,' spluttered the King. 'Ask something else I pray you for the beast is holy and what you desire would be a monstrous sacrilege.'

'I will be content with nothing else,' said Bintnefer stubbornly, 'and I will dine upon the liver of the bull.' Shaking his head with disbelief the Pharaoh reluctantly ordered the bull to be butchered, and that night Bintnefer ate every part of the liver of the bull. Now she thought that Bata was truly dead, little knowing that two great drops of blood had fallen from the carcass at either side of the palace portal.

The next day, the people of the city were astonished to see two towering persea trees overhanging the royal gateway and believed this marvellous growth to be a bountiful omen of future prosperity.

It was not long before the Pharaoh, accompanied by Bintnefer, came to view the trees. Sitting within their shade, the royal couple graciously accepted the acclamations of the people. But the trees whispered into Bintnefer's ear, 'O betrayer, I am Bata and twice you have sought to be rid of me.'

Once again Bintnefer begged a boon from her lover the Pharaoh, 'I desire that the two perseas at the gate be cut down to make fine furniture for my apartments.'

'Ask something else or you will anger me,' cried the Pharaoh.

'My mind is made up,' said the obstinate girl, 'I will see them felled.'

Spluttering with rage at his wilful mistress, the Pharaoh ordered that her wishes be fulfilled. 'But ask me for nothing else or it will go badly for you,' added the monarch darkly. So it was done and to ensure that her desires were fulfilled Bintnefer watched the workmen wield their axes. All at once a tiny sliver of wood flew up and entered her mouth. Gasping with astonishment, the girl swallowed it but then turned her thoughts to the fine furniture that was being constructed for her pleasure.

In the fullness of time, Bintnefer conceived and was raised to the rank of Great Royal Wife. She gave birth to a fine son who was acclaimed the heir to his father the King. Swiftly did he grow, strength and intelligence were his, and when his father passed beyond the Gates of Night he became Pharaoh in his place.

The new Pharaoh commanded, 'Bring to me the sages of the kingdom, the officials, the nobles and the priests, and summon Bintnefer my mother.' As soon as all were assembled the new Pharaoh told them his tale. 'For let none doubt,' continued the Pharaoh, 'that I am Bata, three times slain by this faithless woman. What is to be her fate?'

The wise men, nobles, priest and officials muttered amongst themselves yet the verdict was unanimous. 'Let her be taken and slain for her crimes,' they chorused. And so was it done.

King Bata then sent for his brother Anpu and raised him to royal state. For thirty years did Bata reign and when his days were done and he had gone to dwell in the west, Anpu became Pharaoh ruling over the Two Lands in peace and prosperity.

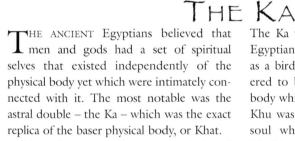

THE KA

THE ANCIENT Egyptians believed that men and gods had a set of spiritual selves that existed independently of the physical body yet which were intimately connected with it. The most notable was the astral double – the Ka – which was the exact replica of the baser physical body, or Khat.

Many funerary practices were designed to ensure that the Ka received the sustenance it required after the body's death, otherwise it could become hungry, wandering the earth as a vengeful spirit. Many of the statues and effigies found in and around tombs were intended as dwelling places for the Ka. It was believed that, with practice, a magician could part his Ka from his physical self to meet with gods, spirits and demons.

The Ka was not the only alternate self in Egyptian belief. The Ba, usually portrayed as a bird with a human head, was considered to be the animating principle of the body which separated from it at death. The Khu was one segment of the imperishable soul while the Sahu was another, the Khaibit was the shadow, while the Ikhu was the breath or vital force.

These seven bodies Ka, Ba, Khu, Sahu, Khaibit, Ikhu and Khat were said to recombine some three thousand years after death thus creating a regeneration of life in the physical world. To ensure that this regeneration took place the corpse had to be preserved by the complex process of mummification and entombment.